Israel 1948:
Countdown To No Where

Don K. Preston D. Div.

Produced by JaDon Management Inc.
1405 4th Ave. N. W. #109
Ardmore, Ok. 73401

Cover Design by: Graphic Designs by Kim
graphicdesignbykim@sbcglobal.net

ISBN 978-0-9799337-9-0

ISRAEL: 1948 COUNTDOWN TO NOWHERE

Don K. Preston D. Div.

ISRAEL: 1948
COUNTDOWN TO NOWHERE

One of the greatest misunderstandings in the religious world today is that the physical nation of Israel remains, as Dwight Pentecost says, "the determinative purpose of God."[1] R. C. Sproul says, "The dramatic return to Palestine of the Jews, and the creation of the state of Israel in 1948, and the recapture of Jerusalem in 1967 have provoked a frenzy of interest in eschatology."[2] Jack Van Impe, on his TV program of 7-17-02, said the restoration of Israel in 1948 is positive proof that we are living in the end times, and that the return of the Lord is at hand.

Tim LaHaye, co-author of the wildly popular *Left Behind* books, and his co-founder of the Pre-Trib Research Center, Thomas Ice, collaborated on a major book *Charting the End Times.* In that work, they claim that the events of 1948 serve to prove that, "Israel, God's super sign of the end times, is a clear indicator that time is growing shorter with each passing hour."[3] We strongly differ with this however, and maintain that 1948 is not related to the time of the end.

What is not commonly known, and there is trouble in the millennial camp about this, is that LaHaye and Ice (hereafter, *Charting*), believe that the Bible predicted *two end time gatherings of Israel*: "We need to be careful to distinguish which prophecies are being fulfilled in our day and which ones await future fulfillment. In short, there will be two end time re-gatherings: one before the Tribulation and one after." (2001, 86)

Charting then cites Arnold Fruchtenbaum to the same effect:

"The re-establishment of the Jewish state in 1948 has not only thrown a monkey wrench in amillennial thinking, but it has also thrown a chink in much of premillennial thinking. Amazingly, some premillennialists have concluded that the present state of Israel has nothing to do with the fulfillment of prophecy. For some reason the present state of Israel does not fit their scheme of things, and so the present state becomes merely an accident....The issue that bothers so

---

[1] J. Dwight Pentecost, *Things To Come,* (Grand Rapids, Zondervan, 1980)471.

[2] R. C. Sproul, *The Last Days According to Jesus,* (Grand Rapids, Baker, 1998)26.

[3] Tim LaHaye and Thomas Ice, *Charting the End Times*, (Eugene, Ore, Harvest House, 2001)85+.

many premillennialists is the fact that not only have the Jews returned in unbelief with regard to the person of Jesus, but the majority of the ones who have returned are not even Orthodox Jews. In fact, the majority are atheists and skeptics.... The real problem is the failure to see that the prophets spoke of two international returns. First, there was to be a re-gathering in unbelief in preparation for judgment namely the judgment of the Tribulation. This was to be followed by a second worldwide re-gathering in faith in preparation for blessing, namely the blessings of the messianic age. Once it is recognized that the Bible speaks of two such gatherings, it is easy to see how the present state of Israel fits into prophecy" (p. 86).

This book will address this vitally important contention, that the Bible predicted two end time gatherings, one in unbelief (1948), and another in belief. We *cannot over-emphasize* how important the events of 1948 are to the millennial scheme. Thus, while our comments will specifically address the claims found in *Charting the End Times*, it needs to be understood that their views are representative of a great portion of the millennial world. To refute *Charting the End Times* is to refute millennialism.

Interestingly, even prominent opponents of dispensationalism seem not to have grasped how important the schema found in *Charting The End Times* is to millennialism, and how devastating it is to show the fallacy of the two re-gatherings doctrine. Even Gentry, in his written debate with Ice, simply commented that a second re-gathering, "will only augment the nation's population."[4] John Bray on the other hand, does briefly discuss the issue, although he does not develop it.[5]

Simply stated, *Charting* is wrong. The Bible did not predict a re-gathering of Israel in unbelief in 1948. And, if we prove this is the case, the *entire millennial house of cards collapses.*

First, we need to address the patently false claim of *Charting*, "It's important to recognize that the capture of the Northern Kingdom of Israel by the Assyrians in the eighth century BC and the captivity to Babylon in

---

[4] Thomas Ice and Kenneth Gentry, *The Great Tribulation: Past of Future?*, (Grand Rapids, Kregel, 1999)174.

[5] John Bray, *Israel in Bible Prophecy*, (P. O. Box 90129, Lakeland Fl. 33804)27, 33.

2

the sixth century BC did not constitute the worldwide scattering mentioned in Bible prophecy. This did not occur until the nation's rejection of Christ and God's subsequent judgment in AD 70" (*Charting*, 85-86). Here is why this is important.

Charting believes that God predicted only two captivities, the Babylonian and the Roman. Sometimes, as in the quote above, they even discount the Babylonian captivity. Thus, if the Assyrian captivity *counts* then their theory is destroyed. There is no place for the return of 1948.

To suggest that the Assyrian and Babylonian Captivities were not the object of prophecy is ludicrous. To suggest that the re-gathering from those captivities was not the object of prophetic concern is a denial of inspired scripture. How did the prophets view these captivities? Let Jeremiah 50:17 answer: "Israel is like scattered sheep; the lions have driven him away. First the king of Assyria devoured him; now last this Nebuchadnezzar has broken his bones."

Were the Assyrian and Babylonian Captivities considered "world-wide" dispersions? Again, allow inspiration to answer. In Deuteronomy 4:25f, the Lord made a prophetic threat to Israel about what would happen when/if they sinned: "When you beget children and grandchildren and have grown old in the land, act corruptly and make a carved image in the form of anything, And do evil in the sight of the Lord your God to provoke Him to anger, I call heaven and earth against you this day, that you will soon utterly perish from the land which you cross over the Jordan to possess; you will not prolong your days on it but will be utterly destroyed. And the Lord will scatter you among the peoples, and you will be left few in numbers among the nations where the Lord will drive you."

Did the Assyrian captivity meet the conditions of this prophecy? The 10 Northern Tribes had lived long in the land. They had made idols for themselves, and became utterly corrupt in the sight of the Lord. The Assyrians then carried them captive into the nations (2 Kings 17). Thus, not only did Israel fit the sinful condition mentioned in Deuteronomy 4, Hosea, writing about the Northern Kingdom described their sin said, "My God shall cast them away, Because they did not obey Him; and they shall be wanderers among the nations" (Hosea 9:17). Patently, the Assyrian captivity was considered a "universal captivity" in spite of the millennial denials. See also Hosea 8:8: "Israel is swallowed up. Now they are among the Gentiles."

Hosea 8:13 is also important. The context is the Assyrian Captivity. However, the prophet says, "For the sacrifice of My offerings they sacrifice flesh and eat it, But the Lord does not accept them. Now He will remember their iniquity and punish their sins. They shall return to Egypt." This reference to returning to Egypt is a clear echo of Deuteronomy 28:68 and the Law of Blessings and Cursings. Jehovah told Israel that if they broke His Covenant they would be scattered to the nations, and He used terminology that was fresh on their minds, He would take them back to Egypt! In other words, any captivity of Israel due to sin was considered metaphorically, a return to "Egypt."

Deuteronomy 28-29 is the blue-print for Jehovah's dealings with Israel. Interestingly, Ice (*Tribulation*, 79) has the temerity to claim that Deuteronomy only records the Babylonian and Roman Captivity. (The astute reader will note that in *Charting*, Ice and LaHaye deny that the Babylonian Captivity was a covenant dispersion!) Thus, they vacillate between positions and contradict themselves. First the Babylonian Captivity was foretold by Moses, but then it is important to understand that neither the Assyrian or the Babylonian captivities really mattered!

However, the prophets directly associated the Assyrian Captivity to Deuteronomy. The chart below will demonstrate beyond doubt that the Assyrian Captivity was anticipated in Deuteronomy. And, this being the case, the contention of *Charting*, is emphatically refuted.

On the left is the passage from the Law of Blessings and Cursings, passages incidentally that Ice claims do not speak of the Assyrian Captivity, but (perhaps) the Babylonian and most assuredly the Roman. The problem is that in Amos, which was a prediction of the Assyrian Captivity, we find unmistakable and undeniable references to the Law of Blessings and Cursings as the reason why the nation was being judged! Was it mere coincidence that Amos cited Deuteronomy? Was he merely using the language of the Law of Blessings and Cursings, but not actually intending to appeal to that Covenant as the ground for the judgment the nation was enduring? This cannot be so, for in the contemporary prophet, Hosea, the Lord reminded Israel that it was her covenant violation that was the cause of her present punishment and Captivity (Hosea 8:12-14).

4

Deuteronomy 28-29	Amos 4-5
28:37- No Bread	4:6- I gave you lack of bread
28:23- No rain	4:7- I withheld the rain
28:22- Blast with Blight	4:9- I blasted you with blight
28:27, 60- I will bring on you the plagues of Egypt	4:10- I set among you the plagues of Egypt
29:23- I will overthrow you as Sodom	4:11-I overthrew you as God Sodom and Gomorrah
28:64/ 28:25- You shall go into Captivity	5:1-5-Gilgal shall go into captivity
They shall return to Egypt (28:68)	They shall return to Egypt (Hosea 8:13).

These parallels are not coincidental, they are precisely the same. Moses threatened Israel with these things if they broke the Covenant. Israel broke the Covenant, and the Cursings of the Covenant came on them, *in the form of the Assyrian Captivity!*

The fact that Amos, Hosea, and Isaiah all posit the Assyrian Captivity as a covenant captivity, as a fulfillment of Deuteronomy 28-30, and a dispersion to the nations, all powerfully refutes the claims found in *Charting*. Their attempt to deny that the Assyrian Captivity was a *prophesied, Covenantal, world-wide* dispersion is theologically derived, not exegetically sound. And make no mistake about it, if the Assyrian Captivity "counts" then the millennial paradigm is doomed!

What then of the Babylonian Captivity? Does it register on the prophetic, covenantal, and world-wide scale? Indeed it does, that is, if we accept the testimony of inspired scriptures.

Consider again Jeremiah 50:17, "Israel is like scattered sheep; the lions have driven him away. First the king of Assyria devoured him; now last this Nebuchadnezzar has broken his bones." Jeremiah knew the significance of what had happened and what was happening, and he knew that the Assyrian as well as the Babylonian Captivity was Covenantal to the core.

Not only did Jeremiah count the Babylonian Captivity as Covenantal, later prophets also saw it as the fulfillment of God's prophetic word.

Nehemiah, recounted Israel's rebellious history, and Jehovah's Covenantal promises:

"We have acted very corruptly against You, and have not kept the commandments, the statutes, nor the ordinances which You commanded Your servant Moses. Remember I pray, the word that You commanded Your servant Moses, saying, If you are unfaithful, I will scatter you among the nations, but if you return to Me, and keep My commandments and do them, though some of you were cast out to the farthest part of the heavens, yet I will gather them from there, and bring them to the place which I have chosen for My Name" (Nehemiah 1:7f).

The historical context here is vital. Israel had sinned and had been scattered to the nations. Now however, the Lord was bringing them back, under Ezra and Nehemiah. The prophet was calling on Jehovah to be faithful to His promises, if the nation truly fulfilled the conditions of the covenant, and repented.

The thing that is vital to see is that Nehemiah appeals to the Mosaic Covenant of Blessings and Cursings. As we have already seen, *Charting* denies that the Babylonian Captivity was prophetically significant. *Charting* denies that Israel had been scattered to the nations. Yet, here was Nehemiah appealing to God for restoration from Babylonian Captivity by direct reference to the Law of Blessings and Cursings. According to *Charting* and Ice (*Tribulation*, 79),[6] this was inappropriate, for Deuteronomy 28-29 was not supposed to predict anything except the Roman Dispersion. If the Babylonian Captivity did not meet the requirements of Deuteronomy, then Nehemiah should not have appealed to it in asking for Jehovah's actions.

Patently however, Nehemiah knew the covenant better than dispensational theologians. He knew that the Babylonian Captivity was included in the Law of Blessings and Cursings. And, since this is true, the teachings found in *Charting* are misleading to say the least.

---

[6] As we have shown, Ice contradicts himself in this regard. In *Charting*, the Babylonian Captivity is not prophetically important. In *Tribulation*, the Babylonian Captivity *is* a covenantal captivity, and must be the critical first one, with the Roman Dispersion being the climactic bondage. This contradiction is important, yet, few seem to notice it.

What we have seen thus far is very destructive to the posit found in *Charting*. There is no justification whatsoever for denying the significance of the Assyrian and Babylonian Captivity. Yet, for the contentions of *Charting* to stand, *they must negate these captivities*. The thing that is so disturbing is that *Charting,* as with LaHaye and Ice in all of their writings, simply makes bold and unsubstantiated claims and expects the reader to accept them without critical thought. This happens repeatedly. We cannot allow such audacious claims to go unchallenged.

A GATHERING IN UNBELIEF: THE EVIDENCE?

What evidence does *Charting* offer to prove that the Bible foretold two gatherings? Specifically, what is the evidence for a gathering in *unbelief*? *Charting* offers several verses: Isaiah 11:11-12, Ezekiel 20:33-38, Ezekiel 22:17-22, Ezekiel 36:22-24, Ezekiel 38-39, and Zephaniah 2:1-2. We will examine each of these texts, and will show that there is no Biblical evidence for a re-gathering of Israel in unbelief. In fact, the very suggestion that God would reward Israel for rebellion, for unbelief, *for sin,* by restoring her to her land, *after first expelling her from that land for unbelief,* is at odds with Truth.

As a primer for this examination, we need to expand and prove that last statement. In Leviticus 26 and Deuteronomy 28-29, we find God's conditions for Israel to dwell in the land, and the conditions for restoration to the land when/if they should be expelled. Simply stated, Jehovah said that if Israel obeyed the Mosaic Covenant faithfully, she could dwell in the land. However, "If you do not obey Me, and do not observe all these commandments...I will do this to you: I will appoint terror over you... I will punish you seven times over...I will bring the land to desolation, and your enemies who dwell in it shall be astonished at it. I will scatter you among the nations and draw a sword after you...those who are left shall waste away in their iniquity in your enemies' lands" (Leviticus 26:14-34).

The condition for restoration to the land is then given,

"But if they confess their iniquity and the iniquity of their fathers, with their unfaithfulness in which they were unfaithful to Me, and that they also walked contrary to Me, then I will remember My covenant with Jacob, and My covenant with Abraham will I remember, I will remember the land" (Leviticus 26:40f).

In other words, if, and when, Israel *repented*, then and *only then* would Jehovah return them to the land. There is not a single word to hint that He

7

would reward their unrighteousness by re-gathering them to the land in their disobedience.

The same is true of Deuteronomy 28-30. Over and over the Lord of Hosts threatened them with captivity and scattering if they violated the Covenant (Deuteronomy 28:36-37; 45-49; 28:64). What is the *only condition* for restoration mentioned in the entirety of the text? It is given in chapter 30:1-10. Three times in the text, Jehovah said that when the plagues and dispersion for sin came upon them, and they would call to mind the Covenant "among all the nations where the Lord your God drives you, and you return to the Lord your God and obey his voice, according to all that I command you today, you and your children...that the Lord your God will bring you back from captivity" (Deuteronomy 30:1-3). Repentance and obedience to the Mosaic Covenant were the conditions for return.

If the reason for *rejection* from the land was rebellion and unbelief, how in the name of reason can anyone posit rebellion and unbelief as a condition for *restoration* to the land?

The interesting thing is that *Charting* claims that Deuteronomy 30 foretold a re-gathering in *belief*. However, you would think that if Jehovah ever had in mind a re-gathering in *unbelief* that He would have included that promise in the covenant. After all, *the covenant is the ground and foundation for the restoration promises.* Thus, if the covenant of Leviticus and Deuteronomy does not contain a promise of a re-gathering in unbelief, then it *is not a covenant promise!*

Finally, it should be noted that when Solomon dedicated the Temple he also took note of the conditions for an eventual return to the land after dispersion and captivity. He said that when captivity occurred, if the people "come to themselves in the land where they were carried captive, and repent, and make supplication...and return to You with all their heart and with all their soul, in the land of their enemies who led them captive," then Jehovah would "hear in heaven, and forgive." (1 Kings 8:45f). Solomon reiterated the conditions of Leviticus and Deuteronomy in asking for a return from dispersion (1 Kings 8:37f). There is not a hint that he thought for a moment that Jehovah would bring Israel out of bondage while they remained in their sin and rebellion.

Does Jehovah *ever* reward sin and rebellion? If the reason for rejection from the land was rebellion and unbelief, how in the name of reason can anyone posit rebellion and unbelief as a prerequisite for restoration to the land? What *Charting* has done is this. On the one hand, they say that Israel was scattered from the land in AD 70 in fulfillment of Deuteronomy 28-29. In other words, Israel was dispersed because of their sin and unbelief. However, *Charting* then turns around and says that in 1948, Israel was re-gathered to the land even though they still maintain their sin and unbelief! No repentance, no change, yet blessed with return!

The millennialists have created a doctrine in which Israel must, in order to enjoy her land, be disobedient and unbelieving. The very reason for her rejection and punishment has now become, ostensibly in 1948, the reason for her blessing! If ever there was a convoluted doctrine, this is it.

THE CONDITION FOR RETURNING

Before proceeding, we must note a vital but overlooked point in regard to Israel's re-gathering. Ice constantly appeals to Deuteronomy 4:25f, and Deuteronomy 30 as containing a divine "roadmap" for God's dealings with Israel (*Tribulation*, 74f). He insists that there will be a future restoration of Israel in fulfillment of these prophecies. We will only address one aspect of this argument, that even Gentry ignored in his otherwise excellent refutation of Ice. That fact is this, in Deuteronomy 30, *no less than three times* Moses said the condition for a return to the land, after dispersion, was for Israel to obey *the Law of Moses*!.

> **If the Mosaic Covenant has been forever removed in Christ, then you cannot say that events 2000 years after its abrogation are the fulfillment of that Covenant!!**

This is where the rub comes in. The Mosaic Covenant, even according to Ice "has forever been fulfilled and discontinued through Christ." (*Prophecy*, 258). Of course, it is interesting that in the same book, just two pages earlier, he said, "In the millennial temple, all that was prescribed and initiated in the Old Testament ceremonial and ritual activities will come to completion and find their fullest meaning." (P. 256). How in the name of reason can one argue that the Mosaic Covenant, with its cultus, has been "completely fulfilled and discontinued in Christ," and then turn around and say that the Old System *will not be completely fulfilled until the millennium?*

Our point is that if the Mosaic Covenant has been, as virtually all millennialists insist, removed forever, then *the divine prerequisite for any return to the land has been removed*, and thus, there cannot be a continuing promise of a return to the land! If God has forever removed the Mosaic Law, obedience to which was the condition for Israel's possession of the land, then even if Israel were to attempt to obey the law it would do no good. It was Jehovah Himself that took away that Covenant with its provisions and promises for return! No obedience, no land. No Covenant, *no promise of return to the land*. And, what this necessitates of course, is that if there is in fact a yet future restoration of Israel then the *Mosaic Covenant has to be restored*. Will the millennialists agree that the Mosaic Covenant has to be restored? How can it be restored if it has been *forever removed*, as Ice says? This is an inescapable problem.

In spite of this undeniable fact, on Saturday afternoon, July 13, 2002, I watched Paul Crouch and his guest on *Trinity Broadcasting*, discussing the events of 1948. Crouch related the joy among the Assembly of God churches in 1948 when Israel was "restored." He said that event was "without a doubt" the fulfillment of prophecy, and then he began a troubled discussion of what "this generation" means. The reason for that discussion of course, is that dispensationalists believe that the generation to see the re-establishment of Israel in 1948 has to be the terminal generation. Crouch noted that Lindsey's prediction of 1988 failed, and that the differing calculations for the duration of a generation are all approaching the terminal point. Not much time is left.

For our purposes, it is significant that *Crouch totally ignored* what *Charting* has attempted to explain, that is, that "the majority of the ones who have returned are...atheists and skeptics." Why would Crouch ignore this? *Because God never promised to return Israel to the land in unbelief.* Crouch knows that those who returned were unbelievers. Thus, he has to ignore the Divinely mandated conditions for restoration, and just insist that 1948 was the fulfillment of prophecy anyway. But this will not work.

If the millennialists are going to claim that 1948 was the fulfillment of prophecy, they must show that Israel met the conditions of Deuteronomy 30, or, that God did predict a return in unbelief. History and the present, proves that Israel was not, and is not, in obedience to the Mosaic Covenant. Thus, Deuteronomy 30 cannot be properly applied to 1948. However, there are no covenantal promises of a return in unbelief, as we will show. Thus, *God's conditions for return have to be ignored when 1948 is discussed.* (Jack Van Impe is a good example. He ignores the conditions of

10

Deuteronomy 30, but claims that 1948 *fulfilled the prophecy.*)[7] Crouch's failure to mention God's conditions for return to the land, while insisting that 1948 was the fulfillment of prophecy, reveals that the millennial camp is turning a blind eye to those conditions. *This is incredibly important.*

We turn now to examine the prophecies that *Charting* offers as proof that Israel was supposed to re-enter the land in unbelief, in 1948.

ISAIAH 11:11-12

We will examine the passages in the order of occurrence in scripture. First, a little anecdote. My father used to tell me that if a person was teaching false doctrine, that you could generally go to the passages they used, and show that they were misusing them. That axiom has proven true, and in the case of a so-called gathering in unbelief, it is surely true.

Some background on Isaiah 11 from the millennial context is helpful to demonstrate the problems of the millennial paradigm. Ice believes that Isaiah 11:1-9 refers to a yet future millennium (*Prophecy*, 1998, 247). This is important, for in verse 10 it says, "In that day there shall be a Root of Jesse, who shall stand as banner to the people; for the Gentiles shall seek Him, and His rest shall be glorious." In other words, the arrival of the so-called millennium of verses 1-9 would result in the raising of the Root of Jesse, *so that the Gentiles could be saved.*

Here is the problem: if the millennium has not come, then the Banner, i.e. the Messiah, has not been raised *so that the Gentiles could be saved.* The text says, "in that day" the Banner would be raised and Gentiles saved. But, "in that day" is still future per the millennialist. Therefore, the salvation of the Gentiles must still be future.

There is a problem here. In Romans 15:8-12, Paul, *the apostle to the Gentiles,* says that Jesus had become the servant to the circumcision, to confirm the promises made to the fathers, *"and that the Gentiles might glorify God, as it is written."* He then quotes four Old Testament prophecies of the calling of the Gentiles, and the last one quoted is Isaiah 11:10.

If Jesus came to fulfill the promises to Israel *so that the Gentiles could be saved,* and if the Gentiles were being saved, then this means that Jesus

---

[7] Jack Van Impe, *Your Future, And A-Z Index to Prophecy*, (Troy, Michigan, Impe Ministries, 1989)70. I have e-mailed and faxed Jack Van Impe no less than four challenges to debate me on the issue of Israel and fulfilled prophecy, and he has not had the courtesy to respond in any way.

11

had fulfilled the promises. But, if Jesus was fulfilling the promises to Israel, so that Gentiles could be saved, *this means that Isaiah 11:10 was being fulfilled.* The problem for the millennialist is that this *demands* that Isaiah 11:1-9 was being fulfilled, because Isaiah undeniably said that *"in that day,"* in the so-called millennium of verses 1-9, the Banner would be raised *so that Gentiles could be saved.* The "in that day" statement of verse 10 is devastating to the millennial view. But, there is more.

Fruchtenbaum says that Isaiah 11:11-12 is actually predictive of a re-gathering in *belief.* However, since Isaiah 11 actually speaks of a gathering *in faith* this supposedly proves a re-gathering in *unbelief.* How does that work? What Fruchtenbaum[8] argues is this: Isaiah predicts a second gathering. This second gathering is of the remnant, and the remnant is *believing Israel.* However, since this is the *second re-gathering,* and it is in *belief,* this must mean that the *first* gathering is in *unbelief.* I have never seen a clearer example of *petitio principii* (begging the question). There is so much presumptuous logic behind this argument that it would take volumes to discount. Nonetheless, we will make an observation or two.

First, the reference here is undoubtedly to the first exodus from Egypt, because the "second exodus" is compared to that event in verse 16. Thus, Isaiah was not dealing with two "last days" gatherings at all. He was speaking of the last days, final "exodus" of the remnant to serve the Lord.

Second, to argue that the second gathering is in faith, therefore the first must be in unbelief is a true "non-sequitur." Why does the first one have to be in unbelief if the second is in belief? Considering the fact that Jehovah clearly, and emphatically said that the condition for return from bondage was belief, there is no justification for projecting a first gathering in unbelief. Can the millennialist produce a single text in the Covenant that suggested a return in unbelief? The answer is an unequivocal No.

In both Leviticus 26 and Deuteronomy 28f, Jehovah clearly stated that the condition for restoration was repentance and obedience, and that those who refused to repent, the rebels, would perish in captivity, and would not return (Leviticus 26:40-45). Now, if there is no provision for a return from captivity in unbelief, the suggestion of such by the millennialist is a theological fabrication without merit.

---

[8] Fruchtenbaum, CTS, Vol. 5, #4, 1999, p. 17. The six part series *Israelology* can be found at: <http://www.e-grace.net/israel.html>.

A final point that needs to be made on Isaiah is in regard to the *Second Exodus*. Scholars have long recognized that Jesus is the Second Moses and that he initiated the Second Exodus.[9] The book of Hebrews develops this theme extensively in chapters 3-4, and the other NT writers use this motif as well. See 1 Peter 2:11-12 for instance.

On Pentecost, as the Spirit was poured out, in the last days, as foretold by Isaiah, Peter's emphatic declaration "this is that which was spoken by the prophet Joel" informs us in no uncertain terms that the time for the anticipated Second Exodus had arrived. It was not an event centuries away. In Acts 2:5f we find that, as Isaiah 11 predicted, there were, "Dwelling at Jerusalem Jews, devout men, out of every nation under heaven," and in the list of nations represented on that Pentecost, it sounds almost like a quote of Isaiah 11:12f. Those who were converted that day were assuredly the remnant of believing Israel, even as Paul affirmed that the remnant was being gathered in his day (Romans 9-11).

The gathering of the remnant concept is one that was special to Paul, and as just stated, a reality in the New Testament. Over and over Paul quoted from Isaiah to refer to the then present work of God gathering the remnant of faithful Israel into Christ. As Isaiah 11 shows, this gathering was to be a last days work of the Messiah. The millennialists says it has not happened, and will not happen until the Tribulation period, and specifically at the *parousia*. For Paul however, the gathering of the remnant, the Second Exodus, was a reality in the first century. To divorce the gathering of the remnant taking place in the first century from the prophecy of Isaiah is to deny the inspired New Testament writers. Their testimony is a clear refutation of the millennial posit of a yet future re-gathering of the remnant, and is especially a rebuttal of the idea of a re-gathering in unbelief.

EZEKIEL 20:33-38

The second text offered by *Charting*, to support the idea that 1948 was a prophesied gathering in unbelief, is Ezekiel 20:33-38:

"As I live, saith the Lord GOD, surely with a mighty hand, and with a stretched out arm, and with fury poured out, will I rule over you:

---

[9] See for instance T. Francis Glasson, *Moses in the Fourth Gospel*, (Napierville, Ill., Alec Allenson Inc.). See also *The New And Greater Exodus: The Exodus Pattern in the New Testament*, Fred L. Fisher, "Southwest Journal of Theology," Vol. 20, 1977, 69+.

And I will bring you out from the people, and will gather you out of the countries wherein ye are scattered, with a mighty hand, and with a stretched out arm, and with fury poured out. And I will bring you into the wilderness of the people, and there will I plead with you face to face. Like as I pleaded with your fathers in the wilderness of the land of Egypt, so will I plead with you, saith the Lord GOD. And I will cause you to pass under the rod, and I will bring you into the bond of the covenant: And I will purge out from among you the rebels, and them that transgress against me: I will bring them forth out of the country where they sojourn, and they shall not enter into the land of Israel: and ye shall know that I am the LORD. (Ezekiel 20:33-38, KJV)

There are several very key things to note about this text.

First, this passage does not mention the "last days." Further, since the historical context of the passage was the impending Babylonian captivity of Judah, we have every right to apply it to that judgment.

Second, as direct support for the first point, the promise/threat of verses 33f, was in response to the sins of Israel, and specifically "you make your sons and daughters to pass through the fire, you defile yourselves with your idols, even to this day" (V. 31). The burning question is, was Israel causing her children to be sacrificed to idols in 1948? Were they worshiping idols in 1948? There is no justification for divorcing the promise of verses 33f from the context of verses 31f, and this means that the promise of verses 33f cannot apply to 1948.

Third, if this passage is predictive of a re-gathering of Israel in 1948, then the re-gathering of 1948 was *a judgment on Israel*, not a blessing to Israel. The language of the text could hardly be clearer: "With a mighty hand, an outstretched arm, and fury poured out, I will rule over you." Now, any way you look at it, that is a *judgment* promise. And, when Jehovah judges someone, that is not good news..

Fourth, if the text is predictive of 1948 then, the literalistic hermeneutic of the millennialists demands that the Lord dealt directly with Israel through his inspired prophet at that time. Note verse 35-36. Jehovah said "And I will bring you into the wilderness of the people, and there will I plead with you *face to face*. Like as I pleaded with your fathers in the wilderness of the land of Egypt." Now, how did *El Shaddai* deal with Israel in the wilderness when He delivered them from Egypt? He did so by means of his inspired, authoritative prophet, Moses. Thus, if 1948 was the fulfillment of this prophecy who was Jehovah's inspired, authoritative

14

prophet? Just how did Jehovah deal *"face to face"* with Israel in 1948? Who was the inspired Moses?

Fifth, the passage emphatically says, "And I will purge out from among you the rebels, and them that transgress against me: I will bring them forth out of the country where they sojourn, *and they shall not enter into the land of Israel:* and ye shall know that I am the LORD." (My emphasis). There could not be a clearer statement, and one more opposed to the millennial view, than this.

Charting **says the unbelievers** *would* **enter the land, Jehovah said the rebels would** *NOT* **enter the land. Who shall we believe?**

It must be remembered that Fruchtenbaum admits concerning those who have immigrated to Israel: "The issue that bothers so many premillennialists is the fact that not only have the Jews returned in unbelief with regard to the person of Jesus, but the majority of the ones who have returned are not even Orthodox Jews. In fact, the majority are atheists and skeptics." Here is the problem.

Fruchtenbaum, Ice and LaHaye insist that the re-establishment of Israel in 1948 is the fulfillment of Ezekiel 20. They insist that Ezekiel predicted a re-gathering *into the land* of unbelievers, and this is the explanation for why the majority of Israeli's today are "not even Orthodox Jews. In fact, the majority are atheists and skeptics."

The problem is that *Ezekiel emphatically says just the opposite.* Jehovah said, "I will purge out from among you the rebels...*and they shall not enter into the land of Israel.*" Now, *Charting* has the rebels, the atheists and agnostics entering the land, but Jehovah said the rebels would not enter the land, *but would be purged from among Israel.* That the rebels, the unbelievers, from among Israel were not purged from their midst is admitted by *Charting.* However, if the rebels were not purged from Israel, and if the unbelievers entered the land, then what happened in 1948 bears no resemblance to the prophecy of Ezekiel 20.

Sixth, in verses 39-40, Jehovah "gave up" on Israel. Why? Because of her *idolatry:* "As for you O house of Israel, thus says the Lord God: Go, and serve every one of you his idols–and hereafter–if you will not obey me: but profane My holy Name no more with your gifts and your idols." Now, if this passage is a prediction of 1948, was Jehovah telling the rebels to worship their idols? This cannot be.

15

Even the millennialists insist that the Babylonian captivity cured Israel of her idolatrous ways. *Charting*, (p. 105) says, "Israel seemed to get the message, (of punishment for idolatry, DKP) for the (Babylonian, DKP) captivity cured them from ever again worshiping idols as a nation." Merrill Unger said: "The Babylonian captivity cured Israel of idolatry"[10] Now, if these statements are true, *and they are*, how can Ezekiel 20:33f, be foretelling 1948? Israel was not worshiping idols in 1948.

The millennialists have misapplied Ezekiel 20 chronologically. They have misapplied it prophetically. There is not one thing in Ezekiel 20 to support a re-gathering of Israel in unbelief, and certainly not in 1948. In fact, the events of 1948 are, as we have just seen, *the total opposite of what Ezekiel predicted*. The same is true of the next passage offered by *Charting*.

Ezekiel 22:18-22

"Son of man, the house of Israel is to me become dross: all they are brass, and tin, and iron, and lead, in the midst of the furnace; they are even the dross of silver. Therefore thus saith the Lord GOD; Because ye are all become dross, behold, therefore I will gather you into the midst of Jerusalem. As they gather silver, and brass, and iron, and lead, and tin, into the midst of the furnace, to blow the fire upon it, to melt ; so will I gather you in mine anger and in my fury, and I will leave you there, and melt you. Yea, I will gather you, and blow upon you in the fire of my wrath, and ye shall be melted in the midst thereof. As silver is melted in the midst of the furnace, so shall ye be melted in the midst thereof; and ye shall know that I the LORD have poured out my fury upon you." (Ezekiel 22:18-22 KJV)

As one examines this passage closely, it becomes painfully evident that *Charting* is grasping at straws, and willing to ignore the context of scripture, all the while constantly claiming that context proves their point. What is the context of Ezekiel 22?

The context is the judgment, not the deliverance of Jerusalem, and specifically, it is the judgment of Jerusalem in BC586. Take note of several things.

First, just like Ezekiel 20, there is no mention of "the last days." There are none of the normal indicators that this is a Messianic prophecy.

---

[10] Merrill Unger, cited by Gentry, (*Tribulation*, 171).

Second, the purpose for this gathering was that *God would judge them.* *Charting* claims that the 1948 re-gathering, "was to be in preparation for judgment" (*Charting,* 86). *This demands that the Tribulation must happen in this generation.* Was God going to gather rebellious Israel in preparation for judgment, and then not bring that judgment for hundreds of years? If the re-gathering of 1948 is indeed the "Super Sign of the End of the Age" per *Charting,* how could that re-gathering be a sign, if what it signified did not occur in close temporal proximity to the sign? *Charting* has, in effect, painted itself into a corner demanding that the Great Tribulation has to occur in the generation that has seen the re-gathering in unbelief.[11]

Third, what was the sin of Jerusalem that was to bring about this gathering, in Ezekiel 22? This is important, because the verses under consideration specifically say that Israel had "become dross to Me." Instead of being precious like gold, silver and precious metal, Israel had become the dross, unworthy of keeping. It was because of her sin that she had become an abomination to Jehovah.

So, what had Israel done? More specifically, what sins was she guilty of that would lead to gathering her to Jerusalem for judgment? This is important, because if verses 18-22 speak of the gathering of Israel for judgment, and if this was predictive of 1948, then we can determine if Israel was truly guilty of the sins described in Ezekiel. If Israel, *in 1948,* was not guilty of the sins for which Ezekiel said she was to be gathered to judgment, then how can it be argued that verses 18-22 speak of the twentieth century? So, we ask again, what sins was Israel guilty of that would lead to gathering her to Jerusalem for judgment?

We find the answer in Ezekiel 22:1-16, and it is not a pretty picture. More importantly, it is not a picture of Israel in 1948. No less than seven times, Jehovah accused Israel *of shedding innocent blood.* Read the

---

[11] This is fascinating since *Charting* chides the attempts of others to say that the Rapture had to occur in this generation, e.g. Lindsay. *Charting,* (p. 37, *Prophecy,* 73) says of Lindsey's calculations in *The Late Great Planet Earth*: "Some start this generation at verse 31 and believe that its talking about the generation beginning at the time Israel became a nation in 1948. The passage of time has disproved that idea." However, if the establishment of Israel in 1948 is the "super sign" of the end, then Lindsey was right after all, or the significance of 1948 is lost with the passing of time.

> To apply Ezekiel 22 to 1948 you must admit that Israel was guilty of shedding innocent blood and idolatry at that time also. For those are the sins for which she was to be gathered.

verses. Who were the innocent that Israel killed prior to 1948? Would that be the Palestinians? To apply Ezekiel 22 to 1948 you must be able to identify the innocent blood Israel had shed. Would *Charting* say that Jehovah actually rewarded Israel with her land in 1948 *for shedding innocent blood?* Would anyone want to affirm that God rewards the shedding of innocent blood?[12] In the New Testament, Jesus and his apostles plainly said that Israel was to be destroyed, in their generation, for shedding the blood of the innocent.

It needs to be understood that the accusation of shedding innocent blood was the charge against Jerusalem in the sixth century BC (e.g. Jeremiah 2, 7, etc.). Thus, the accusation of chapter 22 is not an accusation against 20th century Israel, but against 6th century BC Jerusalem, and her judgment came at the hands of the Babylonians, when Jerusalem was surrounded, pillaged, and destroyed. Ezekiel 22 is not a prediction of 1948.

Another of the accusations in chapter 22 is *idolatry*. See verse 4. Was Israel guilty of idolatry in 1948? See the quotes from millennialists above.

Fourth, verses 17-22 clearly speak of the time of judgment on Jerusalem, and what the millennialists have ignored or overlooked is that verses 3-4 say that *the time of that judgment was near.* "You have become guilty by the blood which you have shed and have defiled yourself with the idols which you have made. You have caused your days to draw near, and have come to the end of your years." It is wrong to take a passage that the prophet applied to his near future, and extrapolate it 2600 years into the future.

---

[12] My book, *Like Father Like Son, On Clouds of Glory*, has a full discussion of the Law of Blood Atonement. Simply stated, according to Numbers 35, there was but one penalty for the purposeful shedding of innocent blood, and that was the death, whether individual or national, of the murderer. Thus, if Israel was guilty of shedding innocent blood, in 1948, but was blessed with a return to the land, in their guilt, it was an unprecedented violation of the Law of Blood Atonement.

Fifth, as suggested already, this gathering was for the purpose of judgment, "So I will gather you in My anger and in My fury, and I will leave you there and melt you." (V. 20). The terms that Jehovah uses for this "gathering" (not *re-gathering*.) cannot be perverted to indicate a blessing from Him. He called Israel "dross" not silver or gold. He said he would blow *fire* on them, in His *wrath* and *fury*, and He would *melt* them. Ezekiel 22 predicted the *destruction*, not the *restoration* of Israel. Did God melt Jerusalem in 1948? These verses speak powerfully of a time, *near to Ezekiel*, of *judgment, fire, wrath and fury* on Israel for her sins of shedding innocent blood and idolatry. To apply this passage to 1948 is a travesty, and a major violation of proper hermeneutics.

> **It is a perversion of scripture to turn God's threat of *destruction* into a promise of *restoration* and blessing.**

EZEKIEL 36:22-24

"Therefore say to the house of Israel, Thus says the Lord God: I do not do this for your sake, O house of Israel, but for My Holy name's sake, which you have profaned among the nations wherever you have went. And I will sanctify My great name, which has been profaned among the nations, which you have profaned in their midst; and the nations shall know that I am the Lord, says the Lord God, when I am hallowed in you before their sight."

It is critical to note the context of this passage.

First, it does not tell us it is a last days prophecy. This is an arbitrary assumption on the part of *Charting*.

Second, if it applies to 1948, then just as in Ezekiel 22, Israel was guilty of shedding innocent blood and of idolatry in 1948. This is specifically identified as the unbelief for which Israel was going to be *punished*, not restored Ezekiel (36:18).

Third, this passage clearly does not refer to a gathering in unbelief, since the promise was, "I will sprinkle clean water on you and you shall be clean, I will cleanse you from all your filthiness and from your idols." This is a promise of a cleansing and healing, not a promise of a gathering in unbelief and atheism.

Let it also be noted that this is a promise *to cure Israel of her idolatrous ways,--* "I will cleanse you of all your filthiness *and your idols*"– (my emphasis). We must remind the reader that the millennialists are adamant

19

that Israel was cured of her idolatry *in the Babylonian Captivity*. See the millennial quotes above. The point is that if Ezekiel 36 predicted that Jehovah was going to cure Israel of her idolatrous ways, and if Israel was cured of her idolatrous ways in the Babylonian Captivity, *there is no justification for applying Ezekiel 36 to 1948.*

Thus, just like the passages we have already examined, Ezekiel 36 gives no support for the millennial view of a re-gathering in unbelief. This passage teaches the direct opposite. It teaches in fact that Israel "will remember your evil deeds, and the deeds that were not good; and you will loathe yourselves in your own sight, for your iniquities and abominations" (v. 31). And, this was the prerequisite for return to the land found in Leviticus 26, and Deuteronomy 30. There is no support for application to this prophecy to the events of 1948 unless one is willing to say that Israel was guilty of idolatry, of shedding innocent blood, and then repented of those crimes. Clearly, that was not the case.

Ezekiel 38-39

Ezekiel 38-39 are two of the most enigmatic chapters in the Bible. To say they are difficult is an understatement of almost humorous proportions. Yet, we can know some things about the text, and more specifically, we can know some things that refute the position found in *Charting*.

The setting for Ezekiel 38-39 is "the latter years" (38:8). Now this can mean one of several things. Sometimes the term is not used as a technical eschatological term. It just means "in the time to come." However, let us grant for the time being that the term latter days as used here is an eschatological referent. To what last days does it refer?

First, it cannot refer to the Christian age *in any way*, because according to the millennialists, the Old Testament *never* spoke of the church age. (*Facts*, 43) Well, if the Old Testament never spoke of the church age in any way, then it follows that Ezekiel 38 has nothing to do with the events of 1948. This is very destructive to the millennial view.

Ice says Ezekiel 38:8 is predictive of *the last days of Israel.(Prophecy*, 10) However, this will not work at all. According to the millennialists, the last days of Israel are the last 7 years of Daniel's Seventy Week countdown, and that last week is not due to begin recounting until after the Rapture when Anti-Christ signs the peace treaty with Israel. *Charting* says this could actually be "days, weeks, months, or even years after the Rapture" (p. 92-93). The point is, how can *Charting* say that Ezekiel 38-39 predicted the events of 1948, when they do not believe that the "last days" foretold

20

by Ezekiel 38-39 were in existence in 1948? This is a huge problem to say the very least. If the last days of Israel do not begin until after the Rapture-- *and only last for 7 years*-- then how can *Charting* say that Ezekiel 38-39, which speaks of *the last days,* was fulfilled in 1948 without thereby demanding that the Rapture took place prior to 1948? This one fact alone destroys *Charting's* claim that Ezekiel 38-39 predicted the re-gathering of Israel, in unbelief, in 1948.

How can *Charting* say that Ezekiel 38-39 predicted the events of 1948, when they do not believe that the "last days" foretold by Ezekiel 38-39 were in existence in 1948?

Second, Ezekiel 39:21-29, is important. Jehovah said: "Now I will bring back the captives of Jacob, and have mercy on the whole house of Israel...they have borne their shame and their unfaithfulness, in which they were unfaithful to Me, when they dwelt safely in their own land." Notice that the Lord once again reiterated the principles and conditions of the Covenant of Leviticus and Deuteronomy 28-30. The condition for a return to the land was repentance and obedience. It was not disobedience.

If Ezekiel 38-39 speaks of the return of Israel, in unbelief, in 1948, it is a clear violation of the Covenant. Even in this text, the prophet said, "The Gentiles shall know that the house of Israel went into captivity for their iniquity; because they were unfaithful to Me." (39:23). Are the nations now, post 1948, to know that Jehovah has restored them *"because* of their atheism and agnosticism," because they are an unregenerated nation that stands in rebellion against His Messiah, and cannot, and would not if given the chance, even worship according to the Old Covenant?

Ezekiel 38-39 offers no support for the contention that 1948 was the fulfillment of prophecy. Specifically, Ezekiel 38-39 not only does not support that idea, it contradicts it in the strongest manner possible. Ezekiel 38-39 has nothing at all to do with the events of the 20th century.

ZEPHANIAH 2:1-2

Thus far, we have seen that *Charting* is guilty of presumptive *eisegesis.* They *read into the text* things that are not only not there, but they deny what is there. This is a very serious issue indeed. Sadly, this practice is clearly evident in their appeal to Zephaniah 2 as a proof that 1948 was the fulfillment of Biblical prophecy: "Gather yourselves together, yes, gather

21

together, O undesirable nation, Before the decree is issued, or the day passes like chaff, Before the Lord's fierce anger comes upon you." (Zephaniah 2:1-2).

First, this prophecy deals with the impending judgment on Jerusalem at the hands of the Babylonians in BC 586. The events were near, "The great day of the Lord is near; it is near and hastens quickly" (1:7, 14).[13] The prediction of Zephaniah applied to the events of his generation and specifically the invasion of Judah by the Babylonians.

Second, the passage does not mention one single thing about Israel already being in captivity due to her sin, and now being re-gathered back to the land. The position of *Charting* demands, however, that Judah would be in captivity, and is now, in chapter 2:1f, in spite of her continued rebellion and disobedience, being re-gathered into the land. This does not work because this book is threatening Judah with exile and destruction, not a re-gathering into the land.

Third, the passage is a "call to assembly" to hear the Lord's call to repentance. In verse three, the Lord says, "Seek the Lord...it may be that you will be hidden from the Day of the Lord." Yet, this does not fit the scenario of *Charting*. their position demands that the re-gathering in unbelief is *preparation of judgment*, not a call to repentance.

Fourth, the Lord told the inhabitants that, "The whole land shall be devoured by the fire of His jealousy. For He will make a speedy riddance of all those who dwell in the land" (1:18). Does this sound like 1948? If so, when were they swiftly *destroyed off the land*? This is not the promise of *restoration from exile*; it is the threat of exile. Once again, Ice and LaHaye turn the text on its head, claiming that it says the opposite of what it actually says.

It is only presuppositional theology that would try to apply Zephaniah to the events of 1948. Such a view violates the fact that this book was written just before the judgment of Judah at the hands of Babylon. It divorces the

---

[13] See my book *Who Is This Babylon* for a fuller discussion of the "Day of the Lord." I show that the Day of the Lord is referent to an in time historical judgment brought about by God's sovereign actions. Anytime He used one army to judgment another country, Jehovah was said to ride on the clouds into that country. He came, with the clouds, with fire, with the shout, etc. This is metaphoric language and was never intended to be taken literally of a visible coming of Deity.

prophet from his time and his world, to speak of times and events totally unrelated to him and his contemporaries.

Clearly, sometimes prophets spoke of things far from their day. However, we know they did, in many cases, because the Lord informed them that their prophecies were not for their day (Numbers 24:17f; Daniel 10:4; 12:4, etc.). There are no such statements in Zephaniah. Instead, the prophet said the Day of the Lord was near. If it was near then, it is not near now. Zephaniah did not predict the events of 1948.

If the events of 1948 are not contained in God's Covenant promises, then the events of 1948 have nothing to do with God's dealings with Israel, for *God is a Covenant keeping God.*

As we close our examination of the passages offered by *Charting* to prove a re-gathering in unbelief, we offer a final thought about the prophets. As the "conscience of the nation," the prophets only reminded Israel of their duty to *keep the covenant,* and Jehovah's faithfulness to the covenant. *They never added new, covenant provisions, because to do so was to bring condemnation on themselves.*

In Deuteronomy 4:2, Jehovah warned Israel: "You shall not add to the word which I command you, nor take from it." This means that the covenant served as the *sole basis* for God's dealings with Israel. Furthermore, Jehovah swore that when He made a covenant, He would not alter that covenant (Psalms 89:34). This means that if the sole covenant provision for a restoration to the land was repentance and prayer, then to provide for a return in unbelief, Jehovah *would have to alter His covenant.*

In Amos 3:7, Jehovah said, "Surely the Lord does nothing unless He reveals His secret to His servants the prophets." As God's spokesmen, the prophets were duty bound *not to add to or take from the covenant.* To do so would be to bring condemnation on themselves. Thus, if the covenant did not provide for a return in unbelief–and it clearly did not- then the *prophets did not predict a return in unbelief.*

23

FULFILLMENT OF PROPHECY
OR NOT THE FULFILLMENT OF PROPHECY???

The question of the significance, or lack thereof, of 1948, needs to be examined briefly, in light of the claims of *Charting*, and the millennial camp represented by that work.

Ice says on the one hand, "The present church age is not a time in which Bible prophecy is being fulfilled." (*Prophecy*, 10). On the next page 11, he says, "It would be too strong to say that there are signs of the end of the church age." *Charting* says, "Prophetic signs relating to Israel are not being fulfilled in our day" (p. 12). Later, they say: "Now, even though the signs of the end times have to do with Israel, we can see that these signs are drawing nearer to fulfillment during the present church age. *So, while Bible prophecy is not being fulfilled in our day,* it is still possible for us to track 'general trends' that set the stage for the coming tribulation, especially since it follows the Rapture" (p. 118).

This position is at odds with the majority of millennialists. Jack Van Impe believes that one has but to read the newspapers to know that the Biblical signs are being fulfilled in our generation. But, not only is *Charting* at odds with most other millennialists, it is contradictory of the other writings by Ice and Tim LaHaye.

In *Charting* (p. 84) it is said, "Israel's re-gathering and the turmoil are *specific signs* that God's end-time program is on the verge of springing into full gear." (My emphasis). On that same page, the heading is *"Israel: God's Super Sign of the End Times."* On page 119, the chapter headline is: *"The Signs of Christ's Return,"* and we find statements like this in regard to the things happening in this generation:

1.) "The first and most important sign, the re-gathering of the Jews in Israel after nearly 2000 years of wandering, is so highly significant that we have devoted one whole chart on that subject alone."

2.) "The rise of Russia to become a world superpower militarily from 1950 to 1995 and beyond is a fulfillment of prophecy."

3.) "All the strikes and unrest we see in the world today are not just a disruption of society, they are a fulfillment of prophecy of the last days."

4.) "The rise of ancient Babylon in our day constitutes another sign of the times that sets the stage." (*Prophecy*, 72)

5.) On page 36 of *Charting* we find this, "What are the signs of the end times? The first sign Jesus pointed to was war. Not just any war, of which the world has seen over 15k to date, but a special war started by two nations and joined by many other nations on either side until all the world is involved. That occurred with the World War I in 1914-1918. Since then there have been *a parade of "signs,"* the most significant one being the re-gathering of the Jewish people back into the land of Israel and the recognition of Israel as a nation in 1948."[14] (My emphasis)

Thus, from affirming that there are no signs being fulfilled in the Christian age, to affirming that there has been a veritable "parade of signs," the authors of *Charting*, present a confused and confusing doctrine. See my book *The Last Days Identified*[15] for an in-depth study of the identity of the last days. In short, the Bible nowhere teaches the end of the Christian age. The Bible doctrine of the "last days" refers to the end of the Old Covenant World of Israel that occurred with the fall of Jerusalem in AD 70.

The question of whether there are signs or no signs of the end of the age is critical to the millennial view. For instance, Ice is adamant, "The Rapture is a sign-less event" (*Prophecy*, 11). However, as we have just seen, Ice and LaHaye are equally zealous in proclaiming that there has been a veritable "parade of signs in our generation."

The normal explanation of this contradiction is to say that there are no signs of the Rapture, but there are signs of the end of the age. Thus, the re-establishment of Israel in 1948 is the "Super Sign of the End of the Age," yet it is not a sign of the Rapture, because, "If there were signs that related to an event (the Rapture, DKP), they would indicate whether it was near or not near. Therefore, the event couldn't happen until after the signs were present, Thus the signs would have to precede the event–which means the event couldn't happen until after the signs appeared. Since the rapture could occur at any moment, it can't be related to any signs at all." (*Prophecy*, 11) Allow me to be blunt, this is *nonsense*.

Ice says that the New Testament writers said the Rapture could occur at any moment, in their generation. It was "imminent, but not near." By this "imminent but not soon" definition, Ice and LaHaye mean that, "If something must take place before an event can happen, then that event is

---

[14] LaHaye originally predicted that the generation that saw *WWI* would see the Rapture. *Beginning of the End*, (Wheaton, Ill, Tyndale, 1972)168f. Like Lindsey, his prediction failed, so he has "re-calculated," and hoped no one would notice.

[15] Don K. Preston, *The Last Days Identified*, (JaDon Management Inc., 2004) Available from my websites.

not imminent. In other words, the necessity of something else taking place first destroys the idea of imminency." (*Prophecy*, 105). Ice then cites 14 New Testament passages that, to him, prove that the New Testament writers believed that the Rapture was "imminent" in the first century. However, *Charting's* doctrine of the restoration of Israel in 1948 totally negates this idea.

> **According to Ice and LaHaye's definition of imminence, the New Testament writers were patently wrong to declare the imminence of the Rapture..**

Was it "prophetically necessary" for Israel to be restored in 1948? And, was that restoration a "Super Sign of the End?" Millennialists, Ice and LaHaye particularly, are adamant that the events of 1948 were an *absolute necessity* in the schema of Jehovah. Well, if this was so, then how did the New Testament writers affirm, no less than 14 times according to Ice, that the Rapture was imminent in the first century? Notice the argument: "The necessity of something else taking place first destroys the idea of imminency"(*Prophecy*, 105). But it was *necessary for Israel to be restored in 1948*, before the Rapture could occur. Therefore, the necessity for Israel to be restored in 1948 destroys the imminence of the Rapture in the New Testament writings. According to Ice and LaHaye's definition of imminence, the New Testament writers were patently wrong to declare the imminence of the Rapture. There is no escape from this conclusion

Finally, consider the inherent contradiction in what Ice and LaHaye posit in regard to signs of the end of the age and the Rapture. On the one hand, they say there are no signs of the Rapture. However, on the other hand, they affirm that the restoration of Israel in 1948 was the "Super Sign of the End of the Age." To say the least, this is a major contradiction.

When do Ice and LaHaye say the Rapture will occur? At the end of the Christian age: "The purpose of the Rapture is to end the church age so that God may return and complete His program with Israel." (*Facts*, 158).

Now, if the Rapture is to end the Christian age, and *if there are signs of the end of the Christian age*, then the signs of the end of the Christian age are, *de facto, signs of the Rapture*. You cannot say that the Rapture and the end of the Christian age[16] are *synchronous* (same time) events, and say that there are signs for one, but not signs for the other. Thus, we say again, if the Rapture is to end the Christian age, and if there are signs of the end of the Christian age, then, it is undeniable that the signs of the end of the Christian age, are *signs of the Rapture.*

This brings us back to the consideration of 1948, and whether it was the fulfillment of prophecy. If God's covenant with Israel made no provision for a return in unbelief, and we have seen that it does not, then it is patently obvious that the events of 1948 were not the fulfillment of prophecy, since: "The majority of the ones who have returned are not even Orthodox Jews. In fact, the majority are atheists and skeptics." However, if the events of 1948 are not contained in God's Covenant promises, then the events of 1948 have nothing to do with God's dealings with Israel, for *God is a Covenant keeping God.* If there is no provision for a return in unbelief, then He would not do it, for it lay outside His Covenant promises.

If 1948 was not the fulfillment of prophecy however, then the entire millennial house of cards found in *Charting* comes tumbling down, for *a return in unbelief is necessary to their schema.* Fruchtenbaum says that an understanding of a gathering in unbelief is vital to solving the conundrum posed by the gathering of "a majority of atheists and agnostics" in 1948. The problem is that, as we have seen, there is not one shred of Biblical evidence to support the doctrine of a re-gathering in unbelief.

To form the argument concisely we would state it thusly:

God made no covenant promises to return Israel to the land in unbelief.

However, the return of Israel in 1948 was a return in unbelief.

Therefore, the return in 1948 was not in fulfillment of God's Covenant promises.

This means that 1948 winds up being totally insignificant prophetically.

> *Prophetically, 1948 is totally insignificant.*

---

[16] The Church age has no end (Ephesians 3:20-21). Thus, for *Charting* to speak of the end of the Christian age is contra scripture.

The reason why 1948 is prophetically insignificant is because, directly contrary to the popular view, *modern Israel is no longer the chosen people of God.* This statement could involve a very lengthy study. However, we will present one brief thought provoking concept for the reader's consideration. Further studies of this important topic are available elsewhere. For the moment, consider the following.

On Wednesday, 3-27-02, a suicide bomber walked into a hotel in Israel and killed himself and over 25 Israelis. This was the latest in a series of escalating attacks against Israel and led to serious retaliation by Israel. What many may be missing, in fact, some will not want to hear, is that the attack that Wednesday, taking place on *Passover*, has tremendous theological implications.

Hal Lindsay insists that Israel remains the chosen people of God. Jim Inhofe, Oklahoma senator, said on the US Senate floor that Israel has the divine right to the land because of Genesis 13. It is no secret that one of the pillars of modern dispensationalism is the view that Israel remains God's chosen, exclusive people.

In 1973 the Arab league attacked Israel on *Yom Kippur*, the Day of Atonement. This is one of Israel's most holy days of the year. It seemed, at first, that Israel was doomed. However, that war lasted, due to Israel's amazing military prowess, only a short time. Millennialists hailed Israel's victory as a positive sign that Jehovah was protecting her, and that, of course, we must be living in the last days. Let's look closer.

Instead of being a proof that Israel remains as God's chosen people, the attack in 1973, and the attack on Passover, proves beyond a shadow of a doubt that Israel is *not* in covenant relationship with Jehovah.

Read Exodus 34:23f: "Three times in the year all your men shall appear before the Lord, the Lord God of Israel. For I will cast out the nations before you and enlarge your borders; neither will any man covet your land when you go up to appear before the Lord your God three times in the year."

The promise here is simple. As long as Israel was in covenant relationship with Jehovah, their enemies would not attack them during their holy feast days. On a recent Trinity Broadcast, I heard Grant Jeffrey saying that, "For 1500 years of Israel's history, there is no record of a single attack against her on any of her Holy Feast Days." Of course, Jeffrey made no mention of the 1973 *Yom Kippur* attack. That would have proven more than a little embarrassing, for his point was to show how God had protected

Israel for so long and his citation of the 1500 years of protection was in that context.

It is important to realize that Jeffrey was (partially) correct. For 1500 years there were no attacks against Israel during her feast days. However, there were notable and highly significant exceptions.

In BC 586 Babylon destroyed Jerusalem, and according to Josephus and other Jewish sources, that happened during the Feast of Pentecost. What is so highly significant is the fact that the prophets of the day, Jeremiah, Zephaniah, etc. clearly enunciated why God was about to send Jerusalem into exile. She had broken her covenant The fall of Jerusalem was proof positive of Israel's alienation from Jehovah.

According to first century Jewish historian Josephus, an eyewitness to the event, the final destruction of Jerusalem in AD 70 also took place during Pentecost, one of Israel's three special feast days. What are the implications of that destruction in light of Exodus 34? Jesus very clearly said the reason Jerusalem was to be devastated in AD 70 was *because of her disobedience* (Matthew 23-24). Specifically, as the early church writers repeatedly observe, Jerusalem was destroyed for crucifying her Messiah.

Furthermore, and this is important, Jesus, and the New Testament writers, claimed that Old Covenant Israel was to be finally cast out in that cataclysm of AD 70. Israel was to be finally cast out, for filling the measure of her sin (Matthew 23:29f; Galatians 4:22f– See my discussion of 2 Thessalonians 1 below for more on this). Her special covenant relationship with Jehovah would be forever terminated. This makes the events of 1973 and the present more significant.

The protective umbrella of Exodus 34 would be removed forever. And, this is particularly important to our present study, because, remember that Ice and LaHaye insist that the Mosaic Covenant has been "forever fulfilled and removed in Christ." Thus, *Charting* cannot argue that the blessings of Exodus have been temporarily set aside, but will one day be restored. If the Mosaic Covenant has been "forever removed" then it will not be restored, but if that protective covenant has been forever removed, then Israel cannot still be God's Covenant people.

The implications of the 1973 *Yom Kippur* attack in light of Exodus 34 are clear and undeniable, therefore. And now, the attack on Passover on 3-27-02. What are the ramifications of this attack, on Israel's Holy Day?

As David said long ago, "By this I know that You are well pleased with me, when my enemies do not triumph over me" (Psalms 41). David's confidence sprang from the promise of Exodus. And yet, the reverse is also true. Anytime Israel was attacked on her Most Holy Days, it meant she was out of relationship with Him.

If Israel is still God's chosen people, that Palestinian bomber should never have been allowed by Jehovah to attack during the Passover. *If Israel is still God's chosen people the attack of 1973 should never have happened.* Instead of Israel's victory at that time being a sign of her elect status, it was, and is, a sign of the direct opposite. It proved, and proves, beyond a shadow of a doubt that the covenantal promise of Exodus 34 is no longer applicable. But if the covenantal promise of Exodus 34 is no longer applicable, then the other promises of that covenant, i.e., the promises of national restoration (e.g. Deuteronomy 30), are also now invalid, abrogated by Jehovah Himself.

Further, the attack on *Yom Kippur* and Passover also prove something else. Either the covenant promise of Exodus 34 is no longer valid, or, *the people claiming to be Israel today are not the people of the covenant of Exodus 34.* If the covenant of Exodus is still valid, but the people in Israel today were attacked in violation of Exodus 34, then what does it say about the identity of the people in Israel today? It says that they cannot be the people of the covenant of Exodus 34.

Every time, and any time, the Palestinians attack Israel during her three feast days, Bible students should be trumpeting the Biblical fact, that this proves, emphatically, *that Israel is no longer the chosen people of God.*

The strange thing is, that even Jewish authorities openly admit that the people calling itself Israel today, are not the descendants of Abraham. John Bray (*Israel*, 44f), has done an excellent job marshaling the evidence, to show that the majority of "Jews" are actually Ashkenazi descent, and that means, unequivocally, that they are of Gentile origin.

The *Encyclopedia Britannica* (1973), Vol. 12, 1054, says, "The findings of physical anthropology show that, contrary to popular view, there is no Jewish race." Jewish scholar and editor, Dr. Camille Honig, said, "it is sheer nonsense...as well as unscientific to speak of a Jewish race." (In Bray, 44). Renowned anthropologist Dr. A. L. Kroeber wrote, "The only fundamentally peculiar element in Zionism is that proponent Jews are not a full nationality and have not been for 2000 years. It is a religion and religious customs...that at the same time held Jews together and segregated them from the rest of the world."[17] This kind of quotation could be

---

[17] Cited in *Whither Israel*, by Cecil Lowry, Ph. D., D. D., "Christians Awake Newsletter," P. O. Box 110013

multiplied many times over. The fact is that the people calling themselves Israel today, are not descendants of Abraham.

The Ashkenazi comprise the majority of Jews today. In the Bible, Ashkenaz was the firstborn son of Gomer who was the firstborn son of Japheth (Genesis 10:3). But, the Abrahamic seed came from *Shem* not Japheth. Furthermore, the Ashkenazi people, who were inhabitants of the territory north of the Caucasian mountains and around the Caspian Sea, were *converts to Judaism in the 8th century*. In approximately 740 AD the king of the Kazars, along with most of the country, converted to Judaism. The *Encyclopedia Britannica* says the facts of this story are "undisputed and unparalleled in the history of central Eurasia." (Bray, 35)

All of the above has tremendous implications. How can one speak of the restoration of Israel, *if Israel ceased to exist in AD 70*, with the fall of Jerusalem and the destruction of the genealogical records? If the majority of the Jews today are of *Gentile lineage*, how can one speak of the events of 1948 as the restoration of the nation of Israel? If the promise of restoration belonged to national, ethnic Israel how then can one apply those covenant promises to those who are not of that ethnic heritage? Judaism today is a religion, or, for the atheists and agnostics that comprise the majority of the country today, a traditional way of life, *not a race of people descended from Abraham*.

West End Station, Birmingham, Ala. No date.

AD 70: DEATH OF OLD TESTAMENT JUDAISM

In harmony with the foregoing, I want to call attention to something that is given precious little attention in the evangelical world, and that is the significance of the destruction of Jerusalem and the temple in AD 70. What follows is an abbreviated form of the material in my book *We Beheld His Glory: A Study of the Transfiguration.*

It is legitimate to question the lineage of those who claim to be Jews today. As seen, even those who call themselves Israelis deny the reality of a Jewish race today. But, what is being missed is that it is even acknowledged, by a variety of sources, that what came out of the destruction of Jerusalem in AD 70 was not anything remotely resembling Old Covenant Judaism. Old Covenant Judaism died in the flames of AD 70.

Following the destruction, a rabbi known as Yohannan Ben Zakkai, who had escaped the cataclysm, approached the Romans and asked permission to establish a school at Joppa. Zakkai realized that with the removal of the temple, priesthood and altar, *Judaism itself hung in the balance.* The fall of Jerusalem in AD 70 was exponentially worse than BC 586. It was truly unparalleled. Judaism itself was in mortal danger.

Realizing that they no longer had access to Jerusalem, with the temple destroyed, the altar turned to chalkstones[18] the priesthood effectively annulled, Zakkai radically transformed Judaism right down to its foundation.

The story of the transformation of Judaism under Zakkai is all but lost on most moderns. It is simply assumed, unfortunately, that modern day Judaism is the Judaism of first century Jerusalem and previous 1500 years. Nothing could be farther from the truth. *It is not too much to say that Old Testament Judaism died in AD 70.* Modern day Judaism bears no resemblance whatsoever to Old Covenant Judaism, and the Jews have recognized, and naturally lamented, this undeniable truth.

---

[18] Cf. Isaiah 27:10-13– Israel's salvation would come at the time when her altar would be turned to chalkstone. This is a common dual motif of judgment and salvation. See my discussion of this prophecy in the *Preston - Simmons Debate* book, available from me at: www.eschatology.org or www.bibleprophecy.com.

> **While most people seem ignorant of the fact, the truth is that *Old Covenant Judaism died in AD 70*. The fundamental transformation of Judaism at the hands of Yohannan Ben Zakkai resulted in the creation of a religion *unknown in the Torah*.**

Berlin and Overman say, "Many have argued that the destruction of the temple in Jerusalem in 70 C. E. constitutes the seminal event in the formation of both early Christianity and Rabbinic Judaism. .... Out of the dust of 70 C. E. Christianity and Judaism as we know them today emerged."[19] Notice the last statements: "the seminal event in the *formation* of Rabbinic Judaism.... Judaism as we know them today."

In similar vein, notice the following:

"The destruction of the Second Temple in 70 C.E. constitutes, in most analyses, a watershed event for the Jews of antiquity. The elimination of the center, source of spiritual nourishment and preeminent symbol of the nation's identity, compelled Jews to reinvent themselves, to find other means of religious sustenance, and to adjust their lives to an indefinite period of displacement."[20]

The same author continues: "The loss of the Jerusalem Temple also meant that the Jewish religion had to transform itself from a Temple-based, sacrificial cult to a culture rooted in domestic and local practices" (*Cultures*, 163). Notice again the terms, "reinvent themselves" and, "find other means of religious sustenance."

As the *Eerdmans Dictionary of Early Judaism* says, Zakkai, "is remembered in rabbinic tradition as having been instrumental in reconstituting Judaism as a viable post-sacrificial religion in the wake of the fall of Jerusalem." They continue by noting that the changes instituted

---

[19] Andrea Berlin and Andrews Overman, *The First Jewish Revolt*, (2002, London and NY, Routledge)5-6.

[20] *Cultures of the Jews: A New History*, David Biale, ed., (New York, Schocken Publishers, 2002)117.

by Zakkai served, "as the foundation for a new post-Temple Judaism."[21] The import of these descriptors cannot be over-emphasized and cannot be ignored. Zakkai reconstituted Judaism, creating a "new Judaism."

One of the fundamental reasons for the willingness to radically transform Judaism at this juncture may well lie in the awful realization on the part of many in Israel, including Josephus and the Rabbis, that the time that their prophecies were supposed to have been fulfilled had come and gone, but Messiah– *per their expectations* – had not come.

Josephus believed that the prophecies of Daniel 9 were fulfilled in the siege and destruction of Jerusalem.[22] He said: "Daniel also wrote concerning the Roman government, and that our country should be made desolate by them." (Antiquities, Bk. X:11, p. 285, Whiston). He saw in the Zealot invasion of the temple the fulfillment of Daniel 9 and the Abomination of Desolation (Whiston, Wars, Bk. IV:5, p. 679ff). Josephus says Daniel fixed the time of the things he foretold, (*Antiquities*, Book X, 13, p. 285, Whiston) and this demands that he was referring to Daniel 9, for as Gaston says: "Daniel 9 is the only passage in the whole Old Testament to give any possibility of predicting the time of the end."[23]

Gaston relates that ben Zakkai, likewise told Vespasian that his rise to power and the impending destruction of Jerusalem was foretold by the scriptures. (*No Stone*, 459).

Gaston relates that Rabbinic understanding of Daniel indicated that Messiah was to come at the time of the destruction of the City and temple, when the sacrifice would be made to cease. Zakkai, as did some other contemporary Rabbis, appealed to Isaiah 10:34 and Zechariah 11:1 as prophecies that were fulfilled in AD 70.

The psychological impact of the destruction was devastating: "Reacting to the destruction of Jerusalem in 70 C. E., Rabbi Simeon states: 'Since the day that the Temple was destroyed there has been no day without its curse;

---

[21] Ra'Anan Boustan, *The Eerdmans Dictionary of Early Judaism*, John J. Collins and Daniel Harlow, eds., (Grand Rapids, 2010)1356.

[22] Josephus also appealed to Vespasian– when Josephus had been captured by him– on the grounds that God had foretold Vespasians' rise to the rule of Rome. (See Whiston, Wars, Bk. III, 8, p. 657).

[23] Lloyd Gaston, *No Stone On Another*, (Leiden, E. J. Brill, 1970)461.

and the dew has not fallen in blessing and the fruits have lost their savour." (Sot. 9:12)." (Cited in Stevenson, *Power and Place*, p. 128).

When Jerusalem fell there appears to have been a widespread realization that something was wrong, horribly wrong. There was, in fact, the realization that *Messiah was supposed to have come in that event*, but that he did not do so, therefore, Israel must now take a new course.

Gaston shares how some Rabbis sought to cope with the disaster. Some took the view that with the fall of Jerusalem: "The coming of the final redemption depended no longer on an apocalyptic plan but only on the repentance of Israel," (Gaston, *Stone*, 464). Likewise, some of the Rabbis said: "All dates for the end have expired and the matter now depends solely on repentance and good works." (Gaston, *Stone*, 464).[24]

Bauckham cites later Rabbinic sources (260 A.D.) that condemn calculations of the time of the end: "Blasted be the bones of those who calculate the end. For they would say, since the predetermined time has arrived, and yet he has not come, he will never come."[25] These rabbis reveal that there was, even in the third century, the realization that AD 70 *was supposed to have been "the end"* but their expectation was disappointed. Thus, they condemned further eschatological investigation.

Do you see how radical the change was? What we have here is nothing less than the psychological abandonment and disconnect from Torah.[26]

---

[24] One can wonder if the "failure" of Messiah to come in the judgment of AD 70 led Rabbi Akiba, a follower of Zaccai, in a bit of desperation, to recognize Bar Kochba as Messiah (circa 134 AD). Could it be that Akiba knew that there were no more possible "dates" and that Bar Kochba offered him the last possible candidate for the Messianic figure? We may never know.

[25] Richard Bauckham, Word Biblical Commentary, Jude, 2 Peter, Vol. 50, (Waco, Word Publishers, 1983)311.

[26] I am not suggesting that Israel as a whole abandoned the prophetic expectation. Some sought to explain the destruction within the context of God's sovereignty and Israel's sin: "Attempts to account for the destruction of the temple (in either 586 BC or 70 CE) typically take two inter-related forms. First the destruction of the temple does not detract from the power of God precisely because it is God himself, not the Babylonians or the Romans, who destroys the

Israel could no longer look to the predictions of their revered prophets. The time predicted by the Old Covenant prophets had come and gone– in the fall of Jerusalem– but Messiah had not come. *The prophecies had failed.* They must re-focus their hope and their direction.

This incredible shift in prophetic understanding, this radical re-evaluation, led to the revolutionary transformation of the body of Israel. After all, if your entire history and identity has been, for almost two millennia, wrapped up in the prophetic expectation of the fulfillment of Torah, and the appointed time for that consummation has come and gone without fulfillment (in the form expected), this failure of fulfillment demanded a radical re-evaluation. It is called *Cognitive Dissonance.*

Simply stated: Cognitive Dissonance is the continued belief in a system or doctrine that has been, for all practical purposes, falsified. So, if, as seems to be the case, the Jewish expectation was that the final salvation of Israel and coming of Messiah was linked to the fall of Jerusalem, and that anticipated salvation did not arrive– per the expectations[27] – then few options remained. Either continue to believe *in spite of the failure*, or, radically transform the entire structure of your beliefs. The latter is what was accomplished under Zakkai .

---

temple and city. Earthly armies are simply the tool of God's divine wrath. Second, blame for the destruction lies at the feet of Jewish unfaithfulness, not God's. The destruction is a manifestation of God's wrath in response to the sin of the Jews." (Stevenson, *Power and Place*, p.160). Yet, it cannot be denied that there was the awful realization that the prophets had set the time for Messiah, i.e. at the destruction of the temple. Jerusalem had fallen as promised, but Messiah and the kingdom had not come *per their expectations.*

[27] That there was a major contrast between Jewish expectation concerning the nature of the "final salvation" the kingdom and the Davidic king is glaringly obvious throughout the ministry of Jesus. They wanted the kingdom to come with observation; Jesus said that was not the nature of the kingdom. They wanted a king on the throne; Jesus rejected their offer of that kingship. They viewed the temple as the necessary symbol of the presence of God; Jesus said "one greater than the temple is here." Failure to see and to honor Jesus' rejection of the Jewish expectation of the kingdom has led to dispensationalism / Zionism in our world.

As the Jews themselves recognize, the tragedy of AD 70 demanded, and Zakkai accomplished: "Judaism had to be recreated for a temple-less and state-less people."[28] Zakkai, "transformed Judaism into a portable religion independent of a temple or specific land."

Gale A. Yee takes note how Rabbi Yohannan ben Zakkai, "in order to ensure the survival of Judaism, completely re-interpreted it. He usurped the priestly authority and placed it with the Pharisees. He usurped the Temple's place and replaced it with the Synagogue. He replaced the sacrificial system with piety and good works: 'Rabbi Yohannon desired not a substitute for the temple and its practices, but a valid equivalent to the Temple."[29] This was / is radical stuff.

At the risk of incurring the displeasure of Zionists, is it not fair to ask whether Israel without temple, altar, priesthood and sacrifice *is actually Old Covenant Israel at all?*

Look at it this way: for almost 1500 years, Israel was identified with, and *as* the Jerusalem temple, the priesthood, the sacrificial cultus. As Biale noted, the temple was "the pre-eminent symbol of Judaism." Now, in AD 70, Israel did not have, and could not have her temple and all of the markers that made her "Israel." So, if the very things that gave you your identity are removed and destroyed, then you are no longer "you."

Thus, when every item that gave Israel her identity was removed, and then, to add "insult to injury" so to speak, a Moslem mosque was built on the ruins of your beloved temple, there could not be a more powerful signal that the Judaism that sprang from Torah, that was commanded in Torah, that was identified in Torah, simply no longer exists. It matters not if a people that calls themselves Israel now possess Palestine. Without her fundamental "markers" that identified her as YHVH's people and city, all removed by YHVH Himself, then Israel is not Israel. See our discussion of circumcision immediately below. From the NT perspective, the singular marker of Israel, identifying her as the chosen seed was removed through Christ's work. Paul's stunning doctrine concerning circumcision was

---

[28] Rabbi Rafi Rank, at http://www.jewishpost.com/archives/rabbis-message/retrieving-the-sceptor.html. Accessed 12-3-10.

[29] Gale A. Yee, *Jewish Feasts And the Gospel of John,* Zaccheus Studies, (Wilmington, Delaware, Michael Glazier, 1989)19-20.

indeed "the offence of the cross" to those in Israel that failed to see that God had always desired the circumcision of the heart, and not the flesh.

What were the Old Covenant markers, identifiers, of Israel if it was not these things? And since– and this cannot be over-emphasized– it was *God Himself* that removed those markers, was He not, in those actions, offering the greatest sign that could be given, *that Old Covenant Israel was no longer His people?*

The end of the temple, priesthood the cultus was a world changing event. Judaism, as it was originally given, and as it had existed for centuries, was gone. Zakkai, hoping to ensure the survival of Judaism, actually transformed the very foundation, the structure, the form, the praxis, the very *identity* of the Jewish religion. He transformed Judaism from the foundations up. This cannot be over-emphasized. Judaism post 70 was not the Judaism of the Old Testament. Zakkai, for all intents and purposes, *destroyed Old Covenant Judaism.*

DeMar is correct when he says: "Jesus' coming to destroy Jerusalem represented the passing of the Old Covenant."[30] The removal of the temple in AD 70 was the consummative removal of Torah itself.

As Boettner (postmillennialist) says, in positing the Jewish War as the time of the Great Tribulation, and the inability of many to grasp that truth, "One reason it is so difficult for some people to realize the Great Tribulation had its fulfillment in the siege and fall of Jerusalem is that they do not fully appreciate what a tremendously important event and what a landmark in history the break-up and abolition of the Old Testament economy really was."[31] Sproul (postmillennialist) adds: "No matter what view of eschatology we embrace, we must take seriously the redemptive-historical importance of Jerusalem's destruction in A.D.70."[32] Coffman (amillennialist) said: "The fall of Jerusalem was the greatest single event of a thousand years, and religiously significant beyond anything else that ever occurred in human history."[33]

---

[30] Gary DeMar, *Last Days Madness* (Revised) (Atlanta, GA., American Vision, 1994)157.

[31] Lorraine Boettner, *The Millennium*, (Philadelphia, Presbyterian and Reformed Press, 1957)203.

[32] R. C. Sproul, *The Last Days According to Jesus,* (Grand Rapids, Baker, 1998)26.

[33] Burton Coffman, *Commentary on 1, 2 Peter,*

The implications of AD 70 for the modern understanding of Judaism, the so-called restoration of Israel and all discussions of a restored temple and cultus are clearly profound. Yet, as we have noted, few commentators are giving the proper attention to these issues.

(Austin, Firm Foundation Publishing,1979)246.

THESE SHALL BE PUNISHED WITH EVERLASTING DESTRUCTION FROM THE PRESENCE OF THE LORD

When I was a young man I heard many powerful lessons based on 2 Thessalonians 1:7f: "To you who are troubled, rest, with us, when the Lord Jesus is revealed from heaven, in flaming fire, taking vengeance on those that obey not the gospel...these shall be punished with everlasting destruction from the presence of the Lord and the glory of His power."

When I was in seminary one of my professors began the course on 2 Thessalonians by saying that the text gave him major problems. When asked why that was so, he responded that when you just read the passage in context, A.) The Thessalonians were being persecuted. B.) Paul promised them relief from that persecution. C.) Paul said that relief would come, "when the Lord Jesus is revealed from heaven."

His problem, he continued, was that it is clear that Jesus did not return and give the Thessalonians that promised relief. No one in the class at the time fully grasped the import of what he was saying. Some even scoffed at the idea that the text said any such thing. (The power of tradition to blind us is a strange thing, is it not?)

In the ensuing years I have come to realize what a "problem" 2 Thessalonians 1 truly is for all futurist eschatologies. My professor was right. In numerous formal debates I have appealed to 2 Thessalonians to prove a first century coming of Christ, and not one of my opponents has offered any kind of solid response. Most have totally ignored the argument.

For brevity, let me outline the issues found in 2 Thessalonians 1. See my book *In Flaming Fire*, for a fuller discussion.

☛ The Thessalonians were, when Paul wrote, being actively persecuted for their faith in Christ. This is undeniable.

☛ Paul said that God would repay their persecutors "with tribulation." Christ was going to give to their persecutors what their persecutors were giving them.

☛ Christ would give the Thessalonians "rest" from the Greek word *anesis*. I have not found a single case in which this word is ever used of "reward" or heaven. It is invariably "relief from pressure." The pressure in

Thessalonians was the tribulation (from the Greek word *thlipsis*, which means pressure).

☞ That promised rest (relief) from persecution would be, "when the Lord Jesus is revealed from heaven, in flaming fire."

Here is *a critical key*: Paul said Christ would repay with tribulation "those who are troubling you." Take note of the present tenses.

Fact: A Man of Sin, from the Eastern European Common Market was not the one troubling, i.e. persecuting, the Thessalonians when Paul wrote.

Fact: A Man of Sin and his minions, based in literal Babylon of Iraq was not, "those who are troubling you" when Paul wrote.

Fact: The Roman Catholic pope was not the entity guilty of being, "those who are troubling you" when Paul wrote.

Fact: The Roman empire was not, "those who are troubling you"[34] when Paul wrote.

Fact: "Those who are troubling you", if we are going to deal exegetically with the text, the context and the facts of history, *were none other than the Jews*. There was no other entity persecuting the Thessalonians.

While it may true that the Jews stirred others up against the church in Thessalonica (Acts 17) at least briefly, the indisputable fact is that it was the Jews who were the movers and shakers of the persecution. They, and they alone, must be identified as "those who are troubling you."

These indisputable facts virtually eliminates all futurist eschatologies as viable doctrines.

Paul was affirming that at the parousia, the Thessalonian church – not some far distant, un-identified church, Christ would give those saints relief

---

[34] The popular view that the Romans were the chief persecutors of the church in the first century is false, as an increasing number of scholars and Bible students are coming to realize.. Robert Briggs, *Jewish Temple Imagery in the Book of Revelation*, Studies in Biblical Literature, Vol. 10, (New York, Peter Lang Publishing, 1999)37 says, "There is no good evidence that any Emperor before Decius (mid-third century) issued a general edict against Christianity." He continues, "The alleged evidence for a Domitianic persecution against Christians turns out on closer scrutiny to be highly nebulous at best and therefore ought to be dismissed as illusory." See my *Who Is This Babylon* for a fuller discussion of this issue.

from Jewish persecution.[35] At his coming, Christ would turn the tables on the Jews, and give to them what they were giving to the Thessalonians: It is a righteous thing with God to repay with tribulation (thlipsis) those who are troubling (thlipsis) you."

Now, not to be facetious, but, unless the Jewish persecutors of the Thessalonians were sending those Christian saints to hell, then, since Paul said Christ was going to give to the Jews, *what the Jews were giving to the Christians*, then we are forced to conclude that Paul was saying that *the persecutors would become the persecuted*. And of course, that is precisely what happened.

The Reformed view, shared by many non-Reformed students[36] of this text suggests that the Man of Sin in 2 Thessalonians 2 is to be none other than the Roman Catholic pontiff. This is clearly untenable, since Paul said that the promised relief from that then *contemporary persecution* would be at the judgment of those "who are troubling you." Clearly, the Roman Catholic church cannot, even in the wildest hermeneutical exercise, be identified as "those who are troubling you."

---

[35] As I document in my *In Flaming Fire* book, 2 Thessalonians 1 is destructive to the dispensational view on many levels. 1.) It is about giving the *church* – which, per dispensationalism is *not even on earth at the time of the Second Coming* – relief from persecution. 2.) It has the Jews as the ones persecuting the church, when per millennialism, it is Israel undergoing persecution at the Second Coming. These are just some of the major problems found in the text.

[36] I was personally raised believing that 1 and 2 Thessalonians foretold the future rise to power, once again, of the Papacy and her bloody pursuit of "true believers." I was convinced that it was the pope that would be destroyed at Christ's second coming at the "end of time." Nothing could be more "non-contextual." This view is a distortion of the context, as Gentry himself recognized, born out of the Reformed conflict with Rome. See Gentry's article at: www.goodbirthministries.com/QA_Historicism-Reformed-Theology.php. Valid on 8-25-09. Gentry now applies 2 Thessalonians 1 to the end of history (having nothing to do with Paul's Man of Sin in chapter 2), and, contra all the creeds, chapter 2 refers to Jesus' AD 70 parousia.

Note that Paul did not say that some future church, in some far distant generation will receive relief from persecution at Christ's coming. He said that the Thessalonians, the ones being persecuted at that time, would be given relief from that persecution, "when the Lord Jesus is revealed from heaven."

So, who was it that was, *at that time*, persecuting the Thessalonians? Let me reiterate that it was not the Romans, the Roman Catholic Church, an unknown leader of a future Common Market. It was some entity that was alive and well and persecuting the Thessalonian church when Paul wrote.

Wright says, "Persecution of Christians did not in fact, initially come from pagans" (Victory, 374). He continues by saying that the (so-called) Domitianic persecution was only a possibility and, "it is only that" in spite of scholarly claims to the contrary.[37] He says, "we do not hear of serious or organized persecution by Gentiles until the second century" (p. 374). He says in fact, "If we want hard evidence of sharp controversy between Christians and Pharisees we are on much firmer ground in A.D. 35 (or 45 or 55), than in A.D. 85." (p. 374). Notice the dates that he gives, puts is squarely in the circa of the situation in Thessalonians.

All of this leads us to consider Paul's words about the punishment to be meted out to those "who are troubling you." The apostles says, "these shall be punished with everlasting destruction from the presence of the Lord, and from the glory of His power" (v. 9). Take a closer look at what Paul says.

He says the persecutors would be cast out, "from the presence of the Lord." He uses the word *apo*, meaning "away from, out from." And he says that those persecutors would be punished by being removed from, away from "the presence of the Lord." The word translated presence is literally "face" from *prosopon*.

So, the Jewish persecutors of the Thessalonians were to be eternally cast out from before the face of the Lord. This is thoroughly covenantal language and should be viewed in a corporate sense. Only Israel is ever said – before the coming of Christ – to dwell in the presence, before the face of the Lord.[38]

---

[37] See my *Who Is This Babylon?* for an extensive discussion and refutation of the Domitianic dating of Revelation. Available at: www.bibleprophecy.com.

[38] A study of "the presence of the Lord" or the face of the Lord, and similar terms in the OT definitely reveals that only Israel, only Israel, dwelt in the presence of the Lord and

N. Nisbett, writing in the 18th century, correctly apprised the meaning of Paul's words: "Destruction from the presence of the Lord, and from the glory of his power' appear to me to have a singular propriety in them, when applied to the ruin of the Jewish nation; for God's presence was the peculiar privilege of that people; which they could only forfeit by their wickedness, and their forsaking of the covenant of their God."[39]

So, Paul affirmed that Israel, as a corporate body,[40] was to be eternally cast out of the presence of the Lord when Jesus came in judgment against her for killing him, killing the prophets, and killing his apostles and prophets. He would come and give the Thessalonians relief from their then ongoing persecution, when he would repay with tribulation those who are troubling you." This means that the "restoration of Israel" in 1948 was not the restoration of Biblical Israel.

---

could therefore, be cast out from His presence.

[39] *The Prophecy of the Destruction of Jerusalem*, 1787, p. 25. Reprinted by John Bray Ministries. Available from John Bray Ministry, P.O. Box 90129 Lakeland, Fl. 33804.

[40] Paul is speaking of Israel *as a corporate body* being cast out forever. He is not saying that individual Jews who would seek to follow Christ could not do so. Failure to understand that Paul and the NT writers so often speak in corporate terms has led to a great deal of unhappy theology.

THE CHOSEN SEED AND CIRCUMCISION

At this juncture, we must take note of a vital issue that is virtually ignored in the modern discussions about Israel and God's promises to her, and that is the subject of *circumcision*. It is all but impossible for moderns to appreciate the passion that this topic generated in the New Testament times. To Christians, circumcision is about hygiene; to the Jews it was about God's covenant. It was about being a child of God, their election by Him. It was about the Land. It was about the Temple. It was *everything*.

What Paul taught about circumcision was considered "the offense of the Cross" (Galatians 5:11), by the Jews and Judaizers.[41] The Jews wanted to kill Paul for what he taught about circumcision. And what did Paul teach? He taught that, "If you become circumcised, Christ shall profit you nothing"; "I testify to every man who becomes circumcised that he is a debtor to keep the whole law"; "In Christ Jesus neither circumcision nor uncircumcision avails anything, but faith working through love" (Galatians 5:2-6). So what is the big deal about this? As just noted, we today cannot easily grasp why Paul's doctrine about circumcision would incite such violent reaction. The reason why we have such a difficult time appreciating this is because we are unfamiliar with the true meaning of *covenant*.

For brevity, we will list just a few of the main themes associated with circumcision in the mind of the Jews.

1.) Genesis 17:7 -14– Circumcision and the Identity of God's People. When Jehovah called Abraham, He made the covenant of circumcision with him. The Lord told Abraham that if anyone born in his house or a slave purchased by any of descendants was not circumcised, "he shall be cut off from the people" (Genesis 17:14). This meant he was to *die*.

Simply stated, no circumcision meant you were not of the Abrahamic seed, and if you were not of the Abrahamic seed, you were "outside." For Paul, prior to Christ, there were only two classifications of mankind, the circumcised and the uncircumcised, and the uncircumcised were, "aliens from the commonwealth of Israel, and strangers from the covenants of promise, having no hope and without God in this world." (Ephesians 2:11f). To put it another way, *no circumcision, no hope.*

---

[41] Judaizers were Christians, both Jews and Gentiles, that taught that Gentile Christians had to keep the law of Moses and be circumcised to be saved (Acts 15:1-2).

Now, if you had been taught, as a people, for 1500+ years that circumcision was a sign of God's covenant with you, to identify you as His, and all of a sudden someone started saying that circumcision now meant *nothing*, how would *you* react? If this act identified you as *a child of God*, blessed above all people and now you were told that it no longer had any special significance in God's eyes, wouldn't you consider that man a heretic, a rabble-rouser and a revolutionary?

2.) Joshua 5 – Circumcision and the Land. As Joshua led the children of Israel to the borders of the promised land, it was realized that the men had not been circumcised. The generation that had come out of Egypt had died out, and had failed to have their sons circumcised. As a result, *Israel could not possess the land*.. Joshua had all of the men circumcised and God said: "This day have I rolled the reproach of Egypt from you" (Joshua 5:9). Now if, even as a descendant of Abraham, you could not possess the land if you were not circumcised, how *incredible* was it for Paul to say, "Circumcision avails nothing." Covenantally, no circumcision meant no land. And now, Paul said circumcision avails nothing. The umbilical cord between circumcision and the Land was being cut by the gospel of Messiah.

3.) Acts 21:27f – Circumcision and the Temple. In Acts, the Jews thought Paul had taken Trophimus, an uncircumcised Greek, into the Temple. A riot broke out, and Paul would literally have been killed on the spot had not the Roman commander rescued him. It will be remembered that although the Romans had removed the authority of capital punishment from Israel prior to this occasion, they had actually made exceptions in cases involving violation of the Temple. Thus, there were plaques placed all around the Temple complex, with inscriptions warning all Gentiles that to proceed past a certain point would result in their death.

The Temple was the most sacred place in the world. It was *the center of the world* for the Jews. The privilege of worshiping there was one of the greatest blessings in the world. Circumcision provided passage into those hallowed courts. Without circumcision, no one could enter its holy gates. *No circumcision, no Temple privileges.*

Considering these facets of Israel's identity, perhaps we can begin to have a basic grasp of the passion with which circumcision was viewed by the Jews of Paul's day. No circumcision placed one outside the covenants, outside the land, outside the city, *outside God's favor.*

Is it any wonder why Paul was considered such a *heretic*? Is it any wonder why the Jews sought to kill him? Is it any wonder why his gospel was such an offense to them? For Paul to argue that true circumcision is now of the heart (Colossians 2:11-12), and belongs to those of *faith*, not of the flesh (Philippians 3:1-3), meant that God's election of national Israel was coming to a close. It meant that Israel was being re-defined along spiritual lines, as hinted at by the prophets, but never grasped by those focused on earthly things. It meant, positively, that the time of fulfillment had come, the time anticipated in Genesis 28 and 49 when the scepter would pass from Judah. This was truly good news, except to those who were mindful of the flesh and who trusted in the flesh (Philippians 3).

What is the implication of Paul's doctrine of circumcision for the belief that national Israel remains God's chosen people? *It is devastating.* For Paul, the Abrahamic seed was now being determined by faith, not by circumcision, "Only those who are of faith are of Abraham"(Galatians 3:6f). *This means that physical circumcision no longer determined if a person was of the Abrahamic line.* How *incredibly* important.

Paul taught that in God's eyes the Abrahamic seed is no longer determined by the flesh and circumcision. How then can one speak of the restoration of national Israel as God's chosen people *without rejecting Paul's gospel?* Talk about a *Replacement Theology!*

Jesus said his word, his New Covenant wherein physical circumcision means nothing, would never pass away (Matthew 24:35). Well, if the gospel of Jesus will never pass away, and if the gospel message is that physical circumcision avails nothing with God, how can one teach that national Israel, identified by circumcision, will be restored? *You cannot restore national Israel-identified by obedience to the Abrahamic Covenant of circumcision--to God's favor without annulling the gospel of Jesus Christ* that says, "Neither circumcision nor uncircumcision avails anything." The choice is clear. Circumcision means *no Christ*,[42] but Christ means *no circumcision.* No circumcision means that all emphasis on ethnic identity, all claims to the Land and all emphasis on the City and Temple is nullified.

Thus, *religiously*, Israel is no longer Biblical Israel, because Jehovah removed the Old Covenant, *along with circumcision*, the sacrifices, the

---

[42] Clearly, what we mean is circumcision for religious purposes, as does Paul. Circumcision for hygienic purposes is totally unrelated to Paul's doctrine, and his teaching should never be used to reject sound medical practice.

temple, the priesthood, in AD 70.[43] And, *ethnically*, Israel is no longer Biblical Israel, because Jehovah destroyed the genealogical records in AD 70, and, the majority of those calling themselves Jews today, are atheists, *or are of Gentile descent.*

To make 1948, or any other modern time, the restoration of national Israel to God's favored position one must be willing to affirm the rejection and replacement of the blood bought gospel of Jesus Christ with the obsolete doctrine of circumcision. It is imperative that the modern evangelical world come to grips with these vital truths. The events of 1948 have nothing to do with Old Covenant Biblical Israel.

---

[43] I cannot over-emphasize the fact that the events of AD 70 were *the acts of Christ*, acting in the judgment authority granted to him by the Father (John 5:19f). Thus, AD 70 must be seen as the actions of God; it was God's will to remove the Temple, the altar, the priesthood and circumcision. When seen as the actions of God therefore, the events of AD 70 take on added significance.

BUT, WHAT ABOUT THE LAND PROMISES?

In response to what we have presented thus far, it may be rejoined, "Okay, so 1948 may not be the specific fulfillment of prophecy, but, someday Israel will be re-gathered because God promised that land to her *forever*. Further, Israel has never really possessed all the land promised to her, so the land promise remains valid, even if 1948 really was not the specific fulfillment of prophecy."

Our comments in regard to whether the people in the land today are even the covenant people of God needs to be considered carefully in regards to this question. If modern Israel is not *covenant Israel*, then the land promises to Israel to not apply to them.

Further, we need to briefly consider the two issues raised above: first, did God ever fulfill His promise to Israel to give them the land, and second, how does the fact that He promised the land to them "forever" play into the current situation?

WAS THE LAND PROMISE EVER FULFILLED?

Several years ago, a friend told me that if I could show him that Israel had ever received the land promise, that he would abandon dispensational premillennialism. He had been tutored by some prominent dispensationalists, and was an ardent believer that 1948 was the fulfillment of prophecy. Let me interject at this point how critical the issue of Israel is to dispensationalism. If national Israel is no longer God's chosen people, *the entire house of dispensationalism crumbles to the ground*. Thus, while this book has focused on the writings of LaHaye, Ice, Van Impe, etc., what we have to say is applicable to the entire world of the modern TV evangelists who trumpet the restoration of Israel. But to return to my story.

My friend's tutors had told him repeatedly that Israel had never received the land, at any time. I will tell you the punch line before we proceed, he abandoned dispensationalism. What is the testimony of scripture in regard to whether Israel ever possessed the land? It is clear and unmistakable, *Israel did possess the land.*

We will demonstrate that the inspired writers said, and Israel believed, that *God kept His land promises to them.* And, this is important, we have statements from different critical periods of time in Israel's history, testifying to the fulfilment of those promises.

PERIOD OF CONQUEST

As Joshua led the children of Israel into the land, and conquered it, we have that record in the book of Joshua. What is most significant is how the inspired leader of God summarized the end of that campaign of conquest. His words are found in Joshua 21:43-45:

> "So the Lord God gave Israel all the land which He had sworn to give to their fathers, and they took possession of it and dwelt in it. The Lord gave them rest according to all that He had sworn to their fathers. And not a man of their enemies stood against them; the Lord delivered all their enemies into their hand. Not a word failed of any good thing which the Lord had spoken to the house of Israel. All came to pass."

Remember, we are dealing here with the *time of the conquest* of the land, and Joshua and the children of Israel. More importantly, the Holy Spirit caused the writer to say that God gave them all the land promised to the fathers. They took *possession* of that land, they *dwelt* in the land as promised, and *not one word* of the promises made to the fathers failed.

If Israel ever felt that God had not kept His land promises, *the inspired writer did not feel that way.* The Spirit certainly knew the borders of the land promise, He knew the nature of the promise (conditional or unconditional), and He knew if God had fulfilled the promises. The undeniable, and inspired statement of Joshua is that God did fulfill the land promise to Israel, and that no part of the land promise was unfulfilled. This needs to be heard and accepted by the evangelical world today.

PERIOD OF THE UNITED KINGDOM

When king David died, Solomon inherited the kingdom, and the inspired writer's description of Solomon's kingdom is important to our study:

> "Judah and Israel were as numerous as the sand by the sea in multitude, eating and drinking and rejoicing. So Solomon reigned over all the kingdoms from the River to the land of the Philistines, as far as the border of Egypt. They brought tribute and served Solomon all the days of his life."

This passage is important, because it is a direct allusion to the Abrahamic Covenant of Genesis. In fact, as DeVries points out, the writer's description of the land ruled by Solomon "comprised an empire far vaster then the 'land' that God had promised Abraham."[44] Thus, inspiration tells us that

---

[44] Simon J. DeVries, *Word Biblical Commentary, 1*

God had been faithful to His promises to Israel. He not only gave them the land, He gave them *more than He had originally promised.*

As we have seen, when Solomon dedicated the Temple he referred back to the covenant of Moses and the promises God made to the fathers. In 1 Kings 8, Solomon spoke of God's blessings on Israel: "Blessed be the Lord, who has given rest to His people Israel, according to all that He promised. There has not failed one word of all His good promise, which He promised through His servant Moses." Thus, Solomon, who the writer says ruled over more territory than even contained in the land promise, dedicates the Temple to Jehovah, and says that not one word of His promises to Israel had failed. Shall we accept his word, or continue to deny that Israel ever received her land promises?

For modern Bible students to argue that Jehovah never kept His land promises to Israel is a denial of the statements in Joshua and 1 Kings. Jehovah had been faithful to His promises. He had given them the land.

POST CAPTIVITY

We come now to consider another statement, made at a critical time in Israel's history, about whether Jehovah had ever fulfilled His promise.

In BC586, the two southern tribes of Judah and Benjamin were carried into Babylonian captivity. At the end of that captivity, Nehemiah the prophet led the Jews back to Jerusalem to rebuild the city and Temple in fulfillment of God's promises. As Nehemiah led Israel back to a proper worship of Jehovah, he recounted her history, and among other things he said this:

"You are the Lord God Who chose Abraham, and brought him out of Ur of the Chaldeans, and gave him the name Abraham; You found his heart faithful before You, and made a covenant with him to give him the land of the Canaanites, the Hittites, the Amorites, the Perizzites, the Jebusites, and the Gergashites—to give it to his descendants. You have performed Your words, for You are righteous."

How much clearer could scripture be? If we were to believe the modern millennial writers however, Nehemiah was simply optimistic, or guilty of writing a rose colored history. But, Nehemiah knew the Abrahamic covenant, and the facts, better than the dispensationalists, and he knew that Jehovah had indeed kept His word.

Kings, Volume 12, (Waco, Word Publishers) 1985)72.

NEW TESTAMENT TESTIMONY

This is confirmed even by the New Testament apostles. When Paul spoke in the synagogue of Antioch of Pisidia, he recounted Israel's history: "And when He had destroyed seven nations in the land of Canaan, He distributed their land to them by allotment." (Acts 13:19). The seven nations represent the nations listed by Jehovah in Genesis 15. Although 10 nations are listed in Genesis, by the fourth generation, the time of Israel's conquest, three of the nations that existed when Abraham received the promise had already been destroyed. The point is that Paul the apostle, standing in front of savvy, knowledgeable Jews, said that God had fulfilled His land promises to Israel. We have not one word that any of them disagreed. Not one of them said, "Now, brother Paul, you know that we are still waiting for Jehovah to fulfill the land promise." Paul knew, and those Jews knew, what modern dispensationalists *need* to know, Israel had been given the land.

How else would the Bible writers have had to express themselves for us to be convinced that God gave all the promised land to Israel? The inspired writers said:

1.) God gave Israel the land *as promised*,

2.) God gave them *all* the land He promised,

3.) God gave the land *in fulfillment of His promise to Abraham*.

4.) Israel had *conquered* the land as promised. They *divided* the land by allotment as promised, and they *dwelt* in the land as promised.

5.) Not one word of His promises failed,

6.) God had manifested His faithfulness by fulfilling the land promises.

Here is a worthy challenge: find one Bible text that says Jehovah had *not* given Israel the promised land. Find even one writer after Joshua, that says, "One of these days Jehovah will finally fulfill His land promises to us." *There are no such statements.* On the contrary, every Bible writer that rehearses Israel's history says Jehovah had given them the land: all the land.

BUT, THE LAND IS ISRAEL'S *FOREVER...ISN'T IT??*

One reason so many people firmly believe that Israel has returned to the land, or one day will, is because God promised the land to her *forever*. And, the thinking goes, if God gave the land to Israel *forever*, then forever means *forever*, right? Well, actually, not necessarily.

First of all, let's take a look at the promise. When Jehovah spoke to Abraham, He told him, "all the land which you see I give to you and your descendants forever" (Genesis 13:15). Thus, there is no question that Jehovah did give the land to Israel *forever*. A similar promise is made regarding Israel in 2 Samuel 7:24, where Jehovah said Israel would be His "very own people" *forever*.

The question is, and this will sound strange to the western mind, what does *forever* mean in the Hebrew Bible?

The word translated as *forever* is the Hebrew word *Olam*, (*Strong's Concordance* reference #5769), and is translated as forever, everlasting, perpetual, and other corollary terms. Gesenius' Hebrew-Chaldea Lexicon of the Old Testament,[45] coded to *Strongs'* #5769, says that *Olam* means "what is hidden; specially hidden time, long; the beginning or end of which is either uncertain or else undefined, eternity, perpetuity." He then proceeds to illustrate that the word does not inherently mean forever, in the sense of endlessness as Western oriented minds tend to think.

The study of *olam* could be a lengthy study, beyond the scope of this small work. However, we will present some ideas that will show that the word *olam*, must not be pressed to mean endlessness when applied to the land and national promises to Israel. And, we will show that *even the millennialists agree with this*, and yet, are inconsistent in their use of *olam*.

The Old Testament used the word *olam* to speak of things that virtually everyone agrees were *temporary*. That means that some *eternal* things, *were intended to cease*.

Before we begin, remember that virtually all dispensationalists agree that the Law of Moses has been *permanently removed*. However, are you aware that the Mosaic Covenant, with its cultus, was to stand *forever*? Let's take a brief walk through the Old Testament to examine some of the *eternal* things *they were to pass away*.

---

[45] *Gesenius' Hebrew-Chaldea Lexicon of the Old Testament*, (Grand Rapids, Baker, 1979)612.

1.) Genesis 17:7-8– God made an everlasting covenant with Abraham to give them the land. Now as we have already seen, the retention and possession of the land was a conditional promise, *that demanded obedience to the Law of Moses.* See our comments above.

2.) Genesis 17:13– Circumcision was to be an "everlasting covenant" between God and Israel. Yet, Paul said that circumcision now means nothing, and, to be circumcised for a religious reason is to lose the benefit of Christ's work (Galatians 5:1-6). Thus, circumcision, though everlasting, has ceased as a theologically significant practice.

3.) Exodus 12:14– Jehovah instituted the Passover as an "everlasting ordinance" (Exodus 12:14). Is the Passover binding today? Not if we accept the New Testament teaching. For the Christian "Christ is our Passover" (1 Corinthians 5:7). Furthermore, he commanded Gentile Christians not to be judged in regard to the Jewish feast days, because they were "shadows of good things that are about to come" (Colossians 2:14f). The Old Covenant Passover has ceased as a mandate of Jehovah because what it typified, the deliverance from sin, death, and bondage has become a reality in Christ.

4.) Exodus 27:21– The statute concerning the care for the lamp stand that stood in the Holy Place was to be "a statute forever to their generations." The term "throughout their generations is the key term here. The idea is that the ordinance would stand as long as Jehovah intended for it to stand.

5.) Exodus 29:9– The Lord promised that the priesthood would belong to the Aaronic family "for a perpetual statute." Yet, the New Testament is abundantly clear that the Aaronic priesthood has been superceded by Christ's superior priesthood, and that in fact, the promise of the Levitical priesthood is now "annulled" (Hebrews 7:12-18).

6.) Exodus 29:28– The law of the heave offering was to be a "statute forever." The same is true of the trespass offering (Leviticus 6:18), the division of the sacrifices to the priesthood (Leviticus 7:34), the provision forbidding the priests to drink wine before serving at the altar (Leviticus 10:9), and a variety of other ordinances concerning the sacrifices and the Temple cultus. Yet, the writer of Hebrews says that the Old Covenant ordinances were only imposed, "until the time of reformation" (Hebrews 9:10). Thus, *eternal statutes* are specifically said to be temporary.

7.) Exodus 31:16– The Sabbath was a "perpetual covenant." Yet, Paul, good Jew that he was, said that Gentile Christians were not to be judged on whether they observed the Sabbaths of Israel, and in fact, when writing to the Galatians, he said, "I am afraid of you, for you observe days, and weeks, and months and years" (Galatians 4:10). The attempt to impose those *eternal* statutes on Christians is condemned.

From these examples it is evident that *forever* does not necessarily mean, without end.[46] The demand that forever means without end, can, in fact, lead to serious problems for the millennial view. Not only were the mandates of the Mosaic Covenant said to be eternal, what many do not realize is that Jehovah placed *an eternal curse on Israel.* Yet, we do not hear the millennialists talking about this.

A PERPETUAL CURSE?

What many well intentioned people do not realize when they make the argument that Israel must still be God's chosen people *forever, is that God also cast them off forever.* However, not only did Jehovah cast Israel off *forever,*[47] He did so in *the Babylonian Captivity.*

In Jeremiah 23:39-40, Jehovah threatened Israel with destruction at the hands of the Babylonians: "I will bring an everlasting reproach upon you, and a perpetual shame, which shall not be forgotten." God threatened to make Israel a perpetual (*olam*) shame and reproach. Not only did He threaten her with perpetual shame, He also said that their sin had kindled His fury, and it would burn "forever" (Jeremiah 17:4).

In other words, God's anger was going to burn against Israel *forever,* and, what this means therefore, if you press the *endless* definition, is that Israel would have to be in bondage endlessly. You see, the expression of God's fury was destruction and captivity (cf. Ezra 10:14). Thus, when Jeremiah said that Jehovah's wrath was going to burn against Jerusalem "forever," that meant they would be in *captivity forever.*

---

[46] We are not suggesting that forever cannot mean endless. However, that concept was expressed by saying something would be "without end" (cf. Isa 9:6-9). Sometimes that thought can also be expressed by contrasting things that do end, with things that are *olam*, although this alone is not definitive.

[47] For brevity, we cannot develop this idea here. See my book *Who Is This Babylon?* for a fuller discussion. In short, Jehovah promised that when Israel had filled the measure of her sin by shedding the blood of the innocent, He would destroy her and create a new people, with a new name, in the new creation (Isaiah 2-4; 65-66). In short, God was going to finally cast off Israel, *endlessly.*

Do the millennialists believe that God has made Israel a perpetual, in the sense of endless, shame and reproach? Do they believe that His fury against them will never be quenched, and that they would be in captivity endlessly? How can this be if they are the "apple" of His eye? How can they be His beloved, above all the people of the earth, if they are in fact, a perpetual shame and reproach? If Jehovah's fury still burns against Israel, then surely, there is no way that she could have been "restored" in 1948.

If the millennialists argue that Israel was to be God's people *forever*, they must also admit that Israel was to be *cursed forever*. It will be rejoined that the curse could be removed if Israel repented. However, as we have seen, the millennialists are insistent that Israel had not repented in 1948. Thus, the *eternal curse* should still be on them. (Let it be *clearly understood* that I do *not* believe that Israel *is* under a curse today. Full covenant wrath was finished in AD 70, and that was the end of that Covenant Wrath. To suggest that Israel remains under a curse today, is to totally misapprehend the nature of God's judgment). Further, if it be argued that the eternal curse could end, then this is a tacit admission that the *eternal relationship* could end. You cannot argue one without arguing the other.

The fact is, the word *olam*, translated as forever, everlasting, etc. cannot of itself, isolated from other evidence, be pressed to prove that Israel remains the chosen people of God, and that the land still belongs to them.

From the evidence above we can see that the Old Testament cultic and sacrificial laws were specifically said to be eternal, perpetual, and everlasting. And yet, the New Testament writers emphatically said those things were *intended to be temporary*. What is more, modern millennialists freely admit that the sacrificial system of Israel has been removed, and will never be restored. Thus, in spite of being given *forever*, it is freely admitted by virtually everyone that the *eternal* Old Law was intended to pass. And, that Old Law was to pass because:

1.) It was only a *shadow* of better things to come (Colossians 2:16-17). See the discussion just below. This is a vital truth being almost totally ignored by the millennial world.

2.) Even though they were *perpetual* ordinances, they constituted a law that could not provide salvation (Hebrews 8:8-13; 10:1-4). In other words, that *perpetual* law was flawed, and thus, *needed* to be replaced.

3.) Although the Old Law was *everlasting*, it was only a tutor, a guardian, of Israel until the Messiah was to come (Galatians 3:23-25). When the object and goal of the Law was reached, the Law was to pass.[48]

Now, if a person can understand how the *everlasting sacrificial system* of Moses has been removed by Christ[49], it should not be too difficult to see that although God gave the land to Israel forever, and chose them as His people forever, that this situation was not intended to last *without end*. When *Israel and the land* had served her divine purpose, and reached her appointed goal in God's scheme, just like when the Temple, the sacrifices, and the Levitical priesthood had served their purpose, then that exclusive, divinely sanctioned status ended. And, the fascinating thing is that the Old Testament anticipated that the time was coming when Israel and the land was going to lose her special position, because her goal had been reached.

We can only briefly note a few passages that suggest that when God's purpose for Israel had been fulfilled, that her special place in the sun, her *eternal* standing, was to cease.

1.) Genesis 28:15f – When Jacob saw his famous dream of the ladder from heaven, Jehovah reiterated the Abrahamic covenant promise to him. Jehovah assured Jacob that he would be with him, and he would fulfill that covenant to him and his seed. He then promised, "I will not leave you until I have done what I have spoken to you."

---

[48] See my *Have Heaven and Earth Passed Away?* for a fuller discussion of the temporary nature of the "eternal" Old Law, and how it was intended to pass when it had accomplished it purposes. In addition, see the *Preston - Simmons* written debate on the passing of Torah. Simmons took the view that the Law of Moses passed at the cross. I advocated the passing of Torah in AD 70. The book is available from both of my websites.

[49] It is legitimate to ask whether the millennialists actually believe that God intended to remove the Old Law at all. After all, millennialists admit that if the Jews had not rejected Jesus, he would have established the kingdom when he came the first time. When the Jews rejected him, it was then and only then that God suspended the kingdom of Israel, and established the church. Thus, had Israel not rejected Jesus, do the millennialists believe that he would have established the kingdom on earth, with Jerusalem, the Temple and its cultus as the continuing locus of divine acceptable worship?

This passage is not speaking about Jacob personally and exclusively. It is speaking of God's faithfulness to the Abrahamic covenant with Israel as a people, and God said He would not leave Israel "until I have done what I have spoken". Just like Paul said that the Old Law had a divine purpose, and that when that purpose was fulfilled the Old Law was intended to pass, Jehovah told Israel that they had a divine place in His plan, and that He would not forsake them as a people until that plan was realized. However, when the goal of that plan did come, He would forsake them as an exclusive people.

2.) Genesis 49:1-2, 10 – Jacob gathered his sons around him and predicted what would happen "in the last days" (v. 1-2). He then gave the famous prophecy of v. 10: "The scepter shall not depart from Judah, nor a lawgiver from between his feet, until Shiloh come, and to him shall be the obedience of the people." Here is a clear-cut statement that when the Messiah came, Judah would lose her sovereignty. Her *eternal* relationship would cease to exist, because Messiah was to rule. (It is almost universally admitted that the scepter passed from Judah in the fall of Jerusalem in AD 70.[50])

3.) Jeremiah 3:16 – In this great passage, Jehovah foretold the time when Israel would worship Him from their heart, and, "they will say no more, 'The ark of the covenant of the Lord.' It shall not come to mind, nor shall they remember it, nor shall they visit it, nor shall it be made any more."

This remarkable prophecy finds its fulfillment in the words of Jesus in John 4, when he spoke to the Samaritan woman, "The hour is coming when you will neither on this mountain nor in Jerusalem, worship the Father" (John 4:21). Jerusalem, and thus *the land*, was to lose its centrality in God's mind. It is of great importance to note that Jesus' words here were spoken well before the Jews rejected Jesus, and his so-called withdrawal of the kingdom offer. This statement was made early in Jesus' ministry, and thus, Jesus' vision of the kingdom was not geo-centric, earth centered and earth bound. This is very destructive to the millennial view.

What we have in these three incredible prophecies, and there are others, is the prediction that the time was coming when the eternal relationship between Jehovah, Israel and the land was going to be annulled. It should be clear that just because the Old Testament said Israel and the land were

---

[50] See my book, *The Last Days Identified* for a complete discussion of all of the key "last days" texts, demonstrating how that term never refers to the last days of the Christian age, or of time. In that book I examine how Genesis 49 lies behind so much of the NT references to the last days.

chosen *forever*, that these promises were of the same nature as the *eternal sacrifices*. Some "eternal things" were destined to end. The reason they were to end was because they were mere *shadows* of better things.

FIRST THAT WHICH IS NATURAL,
THEN THAT WHICH IS SPIRITUAL

As stated earlier, one of the greatest misunderstandings in the religious world today is that the physical nation of Israel remains as God's chosen people. In this view the spiritual body of Christ is an interim measure destined to be replaced by Israel in the millennium. It is ironic, is it not, that the theologians that protest most vehemently against what they call *Replacement Theology*, are in fact, the strongest *advocates* of *Replacement Theology*? The millennialist says *the church will be replaced by Israel*, but condemn the idea that Israel could be replaced by the church.[51]

The problem with *this* Replacement Theology is that it focuses on an *earthly kingdom* just as the Jews did, and of course, that focus led to the crucifixion of Jesus. Make no mistake about this, and ponder it well, modern dispensationalism is the revival, or continuance, of the Pharisaic and Judaistic demand for an earthly kingdom that killed Jesus. Although Jesus warned, "Beware of the leaven of the Pharisees, and beware of the leaven of Herod" (Mark 8:15), it is clear that the modern church has ingested a large dose of that leaven by demanding, as the Pharisees did, *an earthly kingdom*. We should point out that the one thing that the "leaven of Herod" would positively suggest is an earthly kingdom. Thus, Jesus was warning his audience against the search for an earthly kingdom.

The modern dispensationalists would have gladly joined the crowd that eagerly sought to make Jesus their physical king (John 6:15). Yet, *they would have been rejected that day*, along with the Jews. Therefore, since the Jews offered what the dispensationalists desire, and *since Jesus rejected that offer*, it is undeniably true that *Jesus rejected the dispensational view of the earthly kingdom*. What then would have been their attitude toward Jesus, and the kingdom he was offering? Would they then have joined in with that crowd when they later cried, "Crucify him."

---

[51] I demonstrate this fact in my book, *Like Father Like Son, On Clouds of Glory* available on my website: www.eschatology.org.

59

I realize these are strong words, and be assured that it is not my desire to offend. I know that many well-intentioned believers sincerely believe in the dispensational view of things. However, sincerity does not make that doctrine true. The issues here are serious.

Consider this: The Jews wanted the kingdom and Jesus offered the kingdom. The Jews wanted a king and Jesus came to be king. The Jews offered Jesus the kingdom, but *Jesus rejected their offer*. Jesus offered the Jews the kingdom, but *they rejected his offer*. The burning question is *Why?* If the Jews *wanted* what Jesus was offering, why did they reject his offer? If Jesus *wanted* what the Jews offered, why did he reject their offer?

The *only solution* to this is to realize that the Jews were offering the kind of kingdom that *Jesus did not want*, "My kingdom is not of this world" (John 18:36); "The kingdom does not come with observation" (Luke 17:20f). But of course, the Jews wanted a kingdom of "this world," because that is what they desired in 1 Samuel 8, (see below), when they rejected Jehovah's will for His kingdom. Conversely, Jesus was not offering the kind of kingdom the Jews wanted, or else they would have gladly accepted his offer, and *they would never have killed him*. The dispensationalists believe that had the Jews recognized Jesus, he would not have died. But this is a huge problem.

Thomas Ice says, "Israel could have obtained her much sought after messianic kingdom by recognizing Jesus as the Messiah. We all know the sad reality–the Jews rejected Jesus. As a result, the kingdom is no longer near, but postponed." (*Tribulation*, 115) The problem is, *the Jews did recognize Jesus as Messiah, enough so that they offered him the kingdom. But Jesus rejected that offer. Then, and only then*, did the Jews reject Jesus.

Are we to believe that Jesus could not communicate well enough to let the Jews know that he wanted to be a national ruler? Could he not tell them, *as other would be messiahs had done*, "Take up your swords."? Could Jesus not perceive what kind of kingdom they were offering in John 6? Are we, after all, to believe, to borrow some famous words, "What we have here is a failure to communicate"? Are we, after all, to believe that *Jesus did want what they wanted*, and, they wanted what he was offering, but they, nor he, could communicate well enough to make each other understand what was actually being offered? *Was Jesus' rejection by the Jews just a failure to communicate?*

If Jesus was offering what the Jews wanted, an earthly kingdom, and if the Jews were offering what Jesus wanted, an earthly kingdom, there is no explanation for the fact that Jesus rejected the Jewish offer, and for the fact that the Jews rejected Jesus' offer. This can only mean one thing, Jesus was not offering the kind of kingdom the Jews wanted, and since they wanted an earthly kingdom, then this means Jesus was not offering an earthly kingdom, *and this is why they killed him.*

The idea of an earthly, Messianic kingdom is totally contrary to scripture. We can only sketch a few of the reasons why this is true. In my upcoming book *Like Father Like Son, On Clouds of Glory,* we develop this idea at length. For now, we can only list a few of the reasons why the emphasis on the establishment of an earthly kingdom is false.

First, the establishment of an earthly king was a rejection of Jehovah in the first place. When Israel surveyed the nations and desired to be like them, having a king with armies and nationalistic power, Jehovah told Samuel, "They have not rejected you, they have rejected Me." (I Samuel 8). Thus, the desire to re-establish an earthly kingdom, with a physical king on the throne is a rejection of God.

Second, as seen above, when the Messiah would come into his kingdom, *the sovereignty of Judah would pass away* (Genesis 49). This means that the nationalistic expression of the kingdom of Israel would pass, not be restored, with the establishment of the kingdom.

Third, the earthly kingdom of Israel was a shadow of better things (Hebrews 9-10). The earthly was a shadow of spiritual, not other earthly things. The concept that the earthly kingdom has been temporarily suspended, but will one day be restored, means that God has moved from the shadow, to the reality, but will move back to the shadow.. The book of Hebrews establishes without a doubt that the spiritual body of Christ, the church, constitutes the better things foreshadowed by Israel and her Old Covenant praxis. Thus, to remove the body, the reality, to return to the shadows is a violation of this important but greatly ignored truth.

Fourth, as a directly corollary to #3, Paul says that God's method of operation, His *modus operandi*, is to move from the natural to the spiritual (1 Corinthians 15:46). However, the millennial view says that although God has temporarily set aside the shadow world of Israel, i.e. the natural body, and has established the spiritual body of Christ, that He will in fact, set aside the spiritual body, and return to the natural. This is an emphatic denial of inspired words of Paul.

Fifth, as just seen, Jesus flatly rejected the offer of the earthly kingdom. In John 6:15 Jesus perceived that the crowds were "about to come and make him king" *so he withdrew from them.* Now, the crowd wanted a king, and Jesus came to be king. They were offering him the chance to be king of their earthly kingdom, *but Jesus flatly rejected them.* Here is the truth that is so often tragically overlooked, the Jews did not reject Jesus' offer of the kingdom, until Jesus had rejected the Jewish offer of the kingdom. But if the Jews were offering what Jesus came to establish, why would he reject them? And, if he was offering what they wanted, why then did they reject him? The *only solution* to this conundrum is to realize that Jesus did not come to establish an earthly kingdom, then, now, or ever.

Much more could be said about this issue, but, for brevity sake this will suffice to show that the idea that national Israel must be restored is fallacious, and built on a faulty concept of the kingdom of the Messiah. It was never God's intent that the kingdom be an earthly kingdom. To seek to re-establish that kind of kingdom is to once again reject Him.

SUMMARY AND CONCLUSION

We have examined every passage offered by *Charting* as proof that 1948 was the fulfillment of Old Testament prophecies of two re-gatherings of Israel, one in unbelief, and the other in belief. We have found that *not one* of the passages teaches that Israel would ever, at any time, be gathered back into her land in unbelief.

We have shown that their claim that the Assyrian and Babylonian Captivities were prophetically insignificant is a false claim. The prophets cited Deuteronomy and Leviticus as the reason for those captivities, and cited the restoration Covenant as the basis for the return from those captivities. Ice and LaHaye are in violation of the inspired statements of the prophets in this regard.

The divine condition for Israel to be re-gathered *at any time* was for her to remember *the Law of Moses*, repent of her sin and humble herself before the Lord (Leviticus 26; Deuteronomy 28-30). The suggestion that God would actually *demand* that at some point in time, after being dispersed, Israel would still be rebellious and disobedient, for Him to restore them turns the Scriptures on their head.

Furthermore, we have seen *that obedience to the Mosaic Covenant* was the divine condition for any return to the land at any time. However, Christ removed the Mosaic Covenant in AD 70,[52] and thus, the promise to re-

---

[52] See the Preston-Simmons written debate: *The End of Torah: At the Cross or AD 70,* for an in-depth discussion of the time of the passing of the Law of Moses. That debate is available on my website: www.eschatology.org.

gather Israel has been abrogated. It is illogical to claim that promises contained in an abrogated covenant, await fulfillment, *centuries after that covenant was abrogated.* When a covenant is abrogated and removed, it is gone. It's promises and penalties are no longer applicable. Period.

We have seen that modern Israel is not still the chosen people of God. They are not the descendants of Abraham at all. This means that the events of 1948 were not, and are not prophetically significant. Those events have nothing whatsoever to do with prophecy. The "restoration of Israel" in 1948 is not the "Super Sign of the End of the Age" as claimed by *Charting* and other millennialists. The end of the age came in AD 70, in fulfillment of Jesus' predictions in the Olivet Discourse.[53]

We have proven that Paul, in 2 Thessalonians 1 predicted that at Christ's parousia, Israel, the entity identified as "those who are troubling you" was to be eternally cast out from the presence of the Lord. This is the complete falsification of the claims that Israel, Biblical Old Covenant Israel, was restored in 1948.

We have shown that the doctrine of the restoration of national Israel *demands the rejection and replacement of the gospel of Christ,* wherein "neither circumcision nor uncircumcision avails anything." Are those who espouse the restoration of national Israel willing to openly teach the rejection of Christ's gospel? *Will the blood bought gospel be replaced?*

Finally, we have seen that Israel did possess all the land promised by Jehovah. This is undeniable. We have seen also that just because the Bible says the land belonged to Israel *forever,* this does not in and of itself, prove that the land would be theirs endlessly. The Old Testament foretold the time when Jehovah would no longer have an exclusive relationship with Israel. That time came when Messiah fulfilled the prophecies and became King of kings. And, we have seen that to insist that the earthly kingdom of Israel remains as God's determinative purpose is wrong. An earthly kingdom was not, and is not, the focus of God's purpose.

Jehovah never promised to bless Israel in her unbelief. This means 1948 is not the fulfillment of Biblical prophecy. This book then, has demonstrated that one of the supporting pillars of millennialism, found in *Charting the End Times,* is without Biblical merit.

---

[53] See my, *Into All the World, Then Comes the End,* for a fuller discussion of the end of the age in the first century. The book can be purchased from our website www.eschatology.org

> **It is time for someone to say what needs to be said,
> *Left Behind* has left *Biblical Truth* behind.**

Why does the evangelical community continue to support the ministries of LaHaye, Impe, Lindsey, etc., when their predictions of the end have *undeniably* been proven wrong. As seen above, LaHaye said the generation that witnessed *WWI* would be the final generation. Lindsey said 1988 would be the end, and Van Impe's calculations demanded that *1999* was the year of the Rapture. (*A-Z*, 67) LaHaye's prediction failed. 1988 came and went, and 1999 has come and gone, with no Rapture, no Great Tribulation, no Man of Sin, *nothing*.

The July 1, 2002 edition of *Time* magazine featured 13 pages on what they called the "juggernaut" *of the Left Behind* book phenomenon. These books are, "Among the best selling fiction books of our time, right up there with Tom Clancy and Stephen King." The fictionalized story line of these books is based on the false theology of LaHaye, Lindsey, and Van Impe, yet millions have been enthralled, and frightened, by the books. The comparison with King's books is apropos. *Left Behind* is a theological horror story. It is time for someone to say what needs to be said, *Left Behind* has left Biblical Truth behind, and *Charting the End Times*, has mapped a theological course that will result only in disappointment, discouragement, and even skepticism. Millions of sincere believers are being *left behind* to struggle with their fear of the future. The emphasis on 1948 is wrong, because 1948 is not a countdown to the end. *It is a countdown to nowhere.*

ADDENDUM

A closing note here. There is a group of partial preterists who affirm that 1948 was the fulfillment of Biblical prophecy. It was ostensibly the end of the millennium and the end of the times of the Gentiles spoken of in Luke 21:24. McKenzie says, "I believe we are currently in the time at the end of the millennium when the Gog and Magog invasion happens (Rev. 20:7-10)."[54] He says that this invasion "will happen in the not too distant future" (p. 465, n. 78). This suggestion raises several issues:

1.) This view demands the ability to prove that modern Israel is in fact the fleshly seed of Abraham. This cannot be done, as shown above.

2.) It demands that God currently has two chosen covenantal people.

3.) Do those who take this view espouse the Two Covenant view of John Hagee that Israel today remains under the Covenant with God, and that her covenant promises take precedent over the gospel? If not, why not?

If Torah remains valid for Israel, do they need the gospel? Hagee says no. But, if they need the gospel, and must respond to it for salvation, does this not nullify circumcision—and thus, their right to the land? This alone nullifies any claim that 1948 was in fulfillment of prophecy.

4.) Those who take this view must, just like the dispensationalists, prove that God promised, *anywhere*, to restore Israel *in a state of rebellion*. That cannot be done.

5.) This view likewise raises the issue of circumcision addressed above. Is physical circumcision still binding for the Jew today? Does it still guarantee the land? Why was Paul's doctrine of circumcision "the offence of the cross" if in fact he was affirming that it would remain perpetually valid for fleshly Israel, but was nullified only for those entering Christ?[55]

6.) This view demands that Israel's "last days" existed in 1948– and exist today as well. Yet, Deuteronomy 32 posits Israel's "last end" as occurring at the time when the blood of the martyrs would be avenged. Jesus said that would be in AD 70 (Matthew 23).

---

[54] See Duncan McKenzie, *The AntiChrist and the Second Coming, A Preterist Examination,* Xulon Press, 2009)453. Available on Amazon and other retailers.

[55] There clearly was a transitional time in which Torah remained valid, while the New Covenant was being delivered. Yet, during that time, Torah was nigh unto passing (Hebrews 8:13). See the Preston - Simmons debate for a full discussion of this important issue.

7.) Acts 3 posits the "restoration of all things" foretold in prophecy at the time of Christ's parousia. Yet, those espousing the 1948 restoration of Israel actually admit that Christ's second coming occurred in AD 70. If the restoration of all things foretold in prophecy was to be at the second coming (and it was), and if the second coming was in AD 70, per these partial preterists, then 1948 was patently not the fulfillment of prophecy.[56]

8.) If 1948 was the fulfillment of God's promises to Israel, then undeniably, Torah remains valid *in all of its aspects*, including the cultus, animal sacrifices, and circumcision as just noted. Matthew 5:17f cannot be ignored, and Hebrews 9:6-28 proves that Torah would stand, and only stand, until the second coming, which, again, these partial preterists posit in AD 70. To understate the case, this is problematic for that position.

9.) This view demands that Romans 11:25f was either fulfilled in 1948 or remains to be fulfilled in the (near) future.[57] However, the OT prophecies that serve as Paul's source for his prophecy demand an AD 70 fulfillment[58]

10.) Jesus was emphatic: The events of AD 70 was to be when "all things that are written must be fulfilled" (Luke 21:22). Revelation 10-11 is likewise emphatic that the sounding of the seventh trump would be the consummation of all that the prophets foretold, and that would be the time. Since Jesus and John affirm that all prophecy would be fulfilled in AD 70, that leaves no room for fulfillment of prophecy in 1948 or beyond.

These are only a few of the major obstacles to the partial preterist position that the millennium ended in 1948 with the restoration of "Israel." This is an untenable doctrine.

---

[56] See my extensive study of Acts 3 in my *Like Father Like Son, On Clouds of Glory* book. The NT is clear that the restoration of all things would occur at the end of the Mosaic Covenant, and this is devastating to the idea of 1948 being a predicted restoration of Israel.

[57] McKenzie, (*AntiChrist*, 453, n. 14), says, "According to Paul (Romans 11:25-26) physical Israel will be grafted back into the true Israel sometime in the future. I believe this is beginning to happen in our time but will only fully happen after the Gog and Magog invasion (Ezekiel 39:21-29).

[58] See my discussion of Romans 11 in the Preston-Simmons Debate, available at: www.eschatology.org.

9 780979 933790